R. L. Wannaxam
July 1987
Cairo, Erithreria

_____

‖‖‖‖‖‖‖‖‖‖‖‖‖‖‖‖‖‖‖
D1572542

A FEARFUL FREEDOM

A FEARFUL FREEDOM

*The Story of one man's survival
behind the lines in Japanese
occupied Malaya 1942–45*

by

ROBERT HAMOND

Leo Cooper
in association with
Secker and Warburg

First published in Great Britain in 1984 by
Leo Cooper in association with Martin Secker &
Warburg Limited, 54 Poland Street, London W1V 3DF

Reprinted 1984, 1985

ISBN 0-436-19081-8

Photoset in Great Britain by
Rowland Phototypesetting Limited, Bury St Edmunds, Suffolk
and printed by St Edmundsbury Press,
Bury St Edmunds, Suffolk

DEDICATION

To those who died in battle in Malaya and Singapore,
or as prisoners of war in the Far East.

CONTENTS

LIST OF ILLUSTRATIONS

GLOSSARY OF LOCAL TERMS USED

Atap Hut	Wood/bamboo-framed hut thatched and clad with overlapping fronds of palm leaves, dried and worked in a certain way. (Malay. Rumah Atap or Pondok Atap).
Bĕlachan	Fermented fish/prawn paste with an appalling stink and a very strong taste.
Bĕlukar	(Pronounced 'Blooka'). Secondary woods growth which springs up where jungle has been cleared. Dense and stifling under a close canopy, it makes going very difficult although it is not quite impenetrable.
Beri Beri	Vitamin 'B' deficiency disease. Wet form is oedema or elephantiasis. Dry form is a numbness spreading from fingers and toes towards body.
Bertam	A stemless palm 15–20 feet tall and very close growing. The leaf has a spiny stem with spiny leaflets growing off it.
Bukit	Hill.
Changkul	Shaped like an adze, used in Asia for tilling or hoeing ground. Takes the place of the European spade/pick/hoe/fork.
Elephant Grass	A bamboo-like grass, 6–8 feet tall.
Gunong	Mountain.
Ingping	English soldier. (Chinese).
Kampong	Village.
Kempeitai	Japanese security police similar to the German Gestapo.

Kerengga	Red ants which make leaf nests in secondary growth and undergrowth. Their bite is painful.
Kongsi House	Communal house. (Chinese).
Kuala	The mouth or estuary of a river, or the junction of a tributary stream and a river.
Kueh	Generic name for cakes which can be made out of flour including tapioca root flour.
Lalang	Spear grass (*imperata cylindrica*). Sharp-pointed erect grass about 3 feet tall which colonises abandoned cultivated land.
Mengkuang	(Pandanus). A stemless palm which forms dense thickets in swamp or areas liable to flooding. Leaves are stiff and pointed, up to 20 feet long and about 4 inches wide. A row of downward-curving thorns grow on both edges of each leaf and a row of upward-curving thorns run along the centre spine of each leaf. Almost impenetrable.
Nibong Tree	Nibong palm. The growing point (heart) of all palms makes good eating.
Parang	A jungle-slashing knife like a machete.
Rattan	Over twenty varieties of climbing palm which can be split and used instead of rope or string, especially in the construction of huts.
Sakai	A blanket term for various aboriginal tribes who live in deep jungle.
Sampan	Small boat (Chinese).
Sungei	River or stream.
Tanjong (Tg)	Headland.
Ubi Kayu	Root of tapioca. Poor eating except when young, and of low nutritional value as the flour is almost pure starch. Some varieties are poisonous unless reduced to flour.

AUTHOR'S NOTE

Between 8 December, 1941, when the Japanese invaded Malaya, and 15 February, 1942, when they captured Singapore, they inflicted a series of running defeats on the British, Indian and Australian troops opposing them. Inevitably during the confusion of this long retreat in and out of dense jungle, men became detached from their units. Alone or in small groups they struggled to rejoin their comrades and, when they failed to find them, simply to survive.

Most failed even in this. They were either rounded up by enemy patrols or betrayed to them by the local inhabitants; or, if they avoided this fate, sooner or later died of starvation and disease. A handful, however, tougher or luckier, came through; one of these was Private E. J. Wright of the 6th Norfolks, and this is his story.

Why it has not been told before is explained in the epilogue: how I came to write it is another story. It so happened that I too was in the Royal Norfolk Regiment, though in a different battalion from Jim Wright. I shared with him the chaos and despondency of that heart-breaking retreat south through Johore towards the illusory refuge of Singapore.

Thirty years after these events, I was at a reunion of FEPOWs and there met an ex-member of 6th Norfolks, Bert Hall. In the course of conversation he mentioned how, soon after the war, he had come face to face with Jim Wright, an old friend of his who he thought had died during the retreat. Jim, by nature a reticent man, had told Bert something of the three-and-a-half years he had spent behind the Japanese lines, and then, as if the subject was still too painful, had abruptly shut up.

As far as Bert knew, Jim had never told anyone else of his experiences, preferring to try and forget them.

I was intrigued and took Jim's address. Through our regimental records, I discovered that, indeed, No 5776863 Pte Wright E.J. had been posted missing, believed killed, at Rengit, Malaya, on 27 January, 1942; but his name did not appear on the official Roll of Honour issued by the War Office. This substantiated Bert Hall's account, and soon afterwards I went to see Jim Wright.

I found a sturdy, reserved, but friendly man in his late fifties who, after some hesitation, gave me the outlines of his remarkable story: one, I felt, that even at this late date deserved telling. Would he help me to get it down on paper? Because I had also fought in Johore and in the same regiment at the same time, and he felt that I would know what he was talking about, he agreed.

Jim, it turned out, had a phenomenal memory for dates and details; and it was from the notes he provided that I have been able to write this extraordinary story of suffering and survival. In truth, as it unfolded, I found myself becoming totally involved with these young soldiers, sharing their disappointments and despair, their grief at the death of comrades, their rare moments of relief and joy. Most of all, I came to feel unbounded admiration for their courage and resourcefulness, thrown, unprepared as they were, into that strange and dangerous world.

Robert Hamond

PROLOGUE

As the light faded a hush fell over the jungle. Even the cicadas in the undergrowth ceased their frenzied whirring, stopping suddenly as if they had been turned off by a switch.

In the oppressive silence Jim Wright became acutely aware of his utter loneliness. For a moment panic seized him and he wanted to shout and scream, to shatter the quiet all around him and perhaps, by some miracle, to recall his comrades to his help.

But he knew in his heart that they would never come back. It was over an hour now since they had silently abandoned him to his fate, desperately seeking a slender chance of survival for themselves without the crippling handicap of a wounded man who could not walk without help.

During that long hour the stark hopelessness of his predicament had become apparent to Jim, and he realized that his luck of the past week had now run out. Hardly able to move, far less walk, with no weapon, food or water, and completely lost in this seemingly endless jungle, he saw that he had virtually no hope of survival. He was only twenty-three years old. Since he had landed in Singapore, barely three weeks earlier, he had had to endure a succession of nightmare events and narrow escapes from death, and had seen many of his comrades die around him.

In the last glimmer of light he crawled painfully to the foot of a large tree and leaned his back against it. His head ached intolerably and his wounded foot throbbed without pause. He saw that it had bled copiously as a result of his exertions during the day, and his boot was full of blood.

A sense of despair and misery filled his mind. Why bother to struggle, he thought; he would die here anyway so why try to postpone the inevitable? No one would ever find him in this dense undergrowth, not even the natives or the Japanese patrols. Perhaps it would have been better if he had been killed with the others in the ambush; they were beyond all pain now, whereas he would have to endure a lingering and lonely end. He recoiled from the thought of death. Closing his eyes, he tried to shut out his surroundings and force his tired brain to rest.

After a while he shifted his position a little to try and ease the pain which ran up his right leg from the throbbing wound. It was pitch dark now and the jungle had come alive again, full of strange noises and rustlings which seemed menacing and set his nerves on edge. He licked his parched lips with a desperate longing for a drink, but his water bottle was empty.

He moved his position again and the agony of his foot drew an involuntary cry from his dry throat. Mosquitoes were now swarming on him, droning in his ears and biting his hands and face, but he was too exhausted and miserable to care. If there are mosquitoes, he thought dully, there must be water somewhere at hand, but he knew that he could not search for it until daylight and he was now so listless that he felt no enthusiasm for any effort even then.

He turned his thoughts back to his home, because he found this comforting. He pictured his school holidays, spent with his father in the woods of the Heydon Estate. His father and grandfather had spent all their working lives there, as gamekeepers. Jim had learned much from his father, who had taught him to observe the woodland wild life and to find his way about the woods without getting lost. Jim had learned to shoot straight and to set traps for vermin, and he came to love the woods, never minding being alone with the wild creatures.

He wondered what his father would have thought of these Malayan jungles, thick, stifling and sinister, so different from the clean, sweet-smelling woods of Norfolk. He tried hard to picture the advice which his father would have given him in his present situation, but without success.

As those long dark hours dragged slowly by, his utter exhaustion and tormenting thirst made him light-headed and feverish. His mind wandered back and forth until at times he thought that he was at home, and at others that his comrades were still with him. And then the cruel realization that he was alone and in the jungle would return again to his consciousness. Desperately he shut it out and tried to concentrate on thinking of his home and parents. At last, in spite of his pain and discomfort, he sank into a merciful oblivion which gave him some rest.

CHAPTER ONE

Abruptly into Battle

The 6th Battalion, The Royal Norfolk Regiment, in which Jim Wright was serving, was a unit of the ill-fated 18th Division which had sailed from the Clyde late in October, 1941, bound for Egypt. After a long sea voyage via Canada and Cape Town the Division had been diverted to India. Two days out of Bombay the 53rd Infantry Brigade was detached and sent to Singapore.*

By the time the brigade disembarked on 13 January, 1942, Japanese forces had almost reached the State of Johore.

Prior to mid-1941 the defence of Singapore, Britain's main stronghold in the Far East, had been based on the assumption that any enemy attack would come from the sea. To the north China was an ally already at war with the Japanese, the French still held Indochina and Siam was a friendly neutral country. An attack down the Malayan peninsula was, therefore, considered extremely unlikely and, in any case, the jungles of Malaya were deemed to present an impenetrable barrier.

The defence of Singapore was accordingly planned round a strong Navy, based on Singapore, but also co-operating with Dutch naval forces in the Dutch East Indies, shore-based naval guns in emplacements, and a string of airfields throughout the length of Malaya, bombers from which would make a sea-borne attack on Singapore too costly to contemplate.

The Army maintained a small garrison which carried out the ceremonial and internal security duties necessary in peacetime, and sent detachments to Malaya and Borneo.

* See maps pp. 168–171.

When the Japanese invaded Indo-China in July, 1941, Singapore's defence plans were rendered obsolete overnight. The enemy now had a modern naval base and airfields 300 miles from north Malaya and 600 miles from Singapore itself. They then 'allied' themselves by force to Siam and thus effectively controlled road and rail routes running south to Malaya.

This alarming situation necessitated some reinforcement of Singapore and Malaya, though Whitehall and the Government in Singapore were reluctant to admit that a real threat existed. Modern aircraft, tanks and additional naval forces were requested, but Singapore had a low priority compared with other theatres of war. Those armaments which did eventually arrive came far too late to influence the outcome of the battle.

Static defences were not built, because money for their construction was not approved by the Treasury. When funds were eventually released the civilian work force was unwilling to work on defences because of enemy bombing. Also General Percival considered that the building of defences on Singapore Island would lower morale because it presumed the loss of Malaya to the enemy.

Shortly before the Japanese invasion, our army – British, Australian, Indian and locally-raised troops – was deployed in Malaya to meet this threat. Virtually none had trained in jungle warfare and some Indian regiments had not completed even their basic training before being rushed from India. Aircraft were few and obsolete, there were no tanks and field artillery was in such short supply that some regiments had to be equipped with 3-inch mortars instead. Naval forces were outnumbered and out-gunned, especially after the loss of HMS *Prince of Wales* and HMS *Repulse*.

Conversely, the Japanese forces had campaigned for years in China and, prior to the invasion of Malaya, had carried out intensive jungle warfare training in Indo-China. They had tanks, modern aircraft and overwhelming naval support. Even so, Whitehall and the military command continued to underestimate the Japanese capability throughout the battle.

Although disfigured by ruthlessness and an almost manic brutality – the massacre of prisoners and wounded was typical – General Yamashita's campaign was brilliantly planned and executed. Using the jungle to bypass our defensive positions, sometimes landing units by sea behind our lines, he ensured that no defensive position could be held for long and made every tactical withdrawal a costly and perilous operation.

Failure to hold the Japanese attack on the Slim River bridge had left the way open to Kuala Lumpur. Officers and men of 3 Indian Corps had been fighting and moving, by day and by night, for a month. Casualties had been heavy; few of the survivors had enjoyed proper rest or relief in that time and now all were utterly exhausted. General Wavell, Supreme Commander South-West Pacific, therefore ordered General Percival to withdraw 3 Indian Corps to Johore, delaying the enemy advance with light rearguard actions and passing through the dangerous bottle-neck at Yong Peng by midnight on 24 January.

However, unforeseen events now posed a grave threat to this plan. On 15 January the Japanese landed a small force by sea between Muar and Batu Pahat and, the following day, crossed the Muar River in strength. 45th Indian Infantry Brigade, a raw and inexperienced formation, was driven back to Bakri where it tried to re-group and counter-attack. 2/19th and 2/29th Australian battalions were rushed to their aid, arriving just in time to restore a desperate situation.

On 18 January General Percival received some alarming information. The Japanese troops at Muar had been identified as Lieutenant-General Takuma Nishimura's Imperial Guards Division and were supported by tanks and aircraft. Not only were they advancing south towards Batu Pahat and had already put a battalion ashore behind our lines there but they were also forcing 45th Brigade to withdraw eastwards towards Yong Peng. Percival realized at once that if Nishimura were to annihilate 45th Brigade and overrun or bypass 53rd Brigade in the defile nine miles south-west of Yong Peng, he would capture Yong Peng and trap part of 3 Indian Corps before it had completed its withdrawal. The Corps would then be eliminated, squeezed between the crack Japanese 5th Division, which was advancing south from Segamat, and the Imperial Guards holding Yong Peng.

On the west coast units holding Batu Pahat would also be trapped and destroyed, leaving both roads to Singapore open to the Japanese. Furthermore, reinforcements for Singapore were expected during the first week in February; if the Japanese could seize all Johore quickly, the landing of these reinforcements would become difficult if not impossible, and Singapore's defences would be greatly weakened.

There was little that Percival could do except accelerate the withdrawal of 3 Corps by twenty-four hours and exhort all units opposing the Imperial Guards Division to hold their ground as long as possible. He had already committed to battle the newly-arrived 53rd Infantry Brigade and had no further reserves on which to draw.

In the event the Australians and Indians of 45th Brigade fought tenaciously for several days against overwhelming odds and suffered very heavy casualties during their slow retreat from Bakri. But, by 22 January, the enemy had finally trapped them at Parit Sulong; only nine hundred of the four thousand officers and men who had fought so gallantly during the withdrawal succeeded in rejoining our forces; their wounded were later massacred in cold blood, almost to a man.

But 45th Brigade's courageous action had slowed down the Japanese advance, and a further check, while the enemy tried to destroy 53rd Brigade in the defile position, enabled the last troops of 3 Corps to pass safely through Yong Peng at midnight on 23 January. The task of holding the vital defile position for that critical week had been allotted to the 6th Norfolks. It was a harrowing initiation into jungle warfare. Within three days of landing on Singapore Island, the 53rd Infantry Brigade, consisting of 5th and 6th Norfolks, 2nd Cambridgeshires, 135 Field Regiment RA, and supporting units, had been ordered to take up defensive positions in north-west Johore. These battalions were largely composed of young men – average age twenty-one – like Jim Wright, who had hardly ever left their towns and villages in East Anglia, and had no training in jungle warfare. So it was just as well that they had little idea of what lay ahead as, on 16 January, 1942, 6th Norfolks set out for Yong Peng, confident and high of heart.

That night Jim drove his 15cwt lorry, loaded with stores, across the causeway over the Johore Strait, and headed north in convoy. Apart from the flarepath cut by the headlights, he could not see the countryside through which he was passing, but he was aware that he was shut in by tall trees on either side of the road, and that the thick darkness was relieved only by an occasional glimpse of stars through the treetops.

After about two hours the convoy halted and the drivers

jumped down to stretch their legs and have a smoke. The silence was broken only by the ticking of the hot engines and the occasional 'tock tock' of nightjars. Jim noticed how dark it was – much darker than at home. Only the glow of cigarettes and the flickering gyrations of fireflies could be seen. Within minutes the mosquitoes had found them and the men hurriedly rubbed on hands and faces the strong-smelling anti-mosquito cream with which they had been issued. Then whistles blew and the convoy moved off again.

They reached Ayer Hitam, the site of HQ 53 Brigade, at dawn and, after a short break, drove on to Yong Peng where they turned south-west along the road towards Muar. Nine miles from Yong Peng they came to the area which they were to defend. The road ran through a narrow defile, flanked to the north by Bukit Belah and to the south by Bukit Pelandok. Both hills rose steeply from the road and were covered with dense scrub jungle which made movement difficult and reduced visibility to a few yards.

Jim drove his truck into the vehicle park in a rubber plantation and camouflaged it. Then he set to work feverishly with the other drivers to dig slit-trenches as they had been told that the Japanese had broken through the Brigade which was withdrawing from Muar and were expected to attack the 6th Norfolks some time that day. Fortunately this attack did not take place, although enemy reconnaissance aircraft circled overhead. By dusk the Norfolks had dug their slit-trenches and settled into their positions.

Their first night in the jungle was not restful; the darkness under the trees seemed impenetrable and was full of weird noises which suggested to the newcomers that the Japanese were all around them. This unease, and the attentions of myriads of mosquitoes, made sleep impossible and dawn on 18 January came as a relief to everyone.

During the afternoon the drivers returned to Ayer Hitam to collect stores. On the return journey they were nearing Battalion HQ when several enemy aircraft came in low and attacked them with bombs. They jumped out of their vehicles and dashed for cover, Jim plunging into a swamp up to his waist. After the raid he saw that some of his comrades had been killed, including a ginger-haired man who had won at his weight in the boxing matches held in the ship. This first sight of dead bodies made Jim feel physically sick and brought home to him forcibly for the first time that he really was at war.

Another restless night passed and in the morning Jim made two journeys to Parit Sulong to collect wounded Australian and Indian troops whom he ferried back to Yong Peng. He had only just returned to the vehicle park and was about to get his meal when the Japanese attacked Bukit Pelandok, overrunning C Company and capturing the hill. As soon as he heard the firing, Jim seized his rifle and jumped into his slit-trench. Before long several men from C Company appeared; some were supporting walking wounded and many were in a state of shock and incoherence. Jim gathered that the enemy had burst out of the dense thickets on the hill, screaming and shouting, and had taken them completely by surprise. He felt a cold stab of fear as he realized that the Japanese were now only a few hundred yards away. Later reports that they had also infiltrated behind D Company's positions did nothing to allay his anxiety.

During the night he was woken by shouts and firing. He strained his eyes to pierce the darkness, fully expecting the Japanese to appear at any moment. But eventually the firing died away and he learned later that the enemy had attacked a convoy of ambulances from Parit Sulong just as it passed through D Company's road block, but had been beaten back.

At dawn on 20 January Jim watched the 3/16th Punjab Regiment put in an attack on Bukit Belah. The summit of this hill was still held by D Company, which was effectively cut off from Battalion HQ. The attack was a disaster; Lieutenant-Colonel H. D. Moorhead, who had led the Punjabis so gallantly throughout the length of Malaya, was killed; his leading company was wiped out and D Company, 6th Norfolks, was finally overrun by the enemy. A counter-attack by B Company later in the day failed to dislodge the Japanese.

For the next thirty-six hours the enemy limited themselves to patrolling, but this was enough to deprive the defenders of any chance of sleep. During this period Jim made several journeys back to Yong Peng and Ayer Hitam and brought ammunition up to the forward companies. He noticed that all the men looked desperately tired, although neither he nor they were really aware of the great danger in which the Japanese successes had placed them.

By the morning of 23 January it was evident that the defile

position could no longer be held against a determined attack, and it was a great relief when orders were given to withdraw to Ayer Hitam during the afternoon and evening of that day. All hoped fervently that the Japanese would not attack during the withdrawal because the road back to Yong Peng ran for nearly two miles along an exposed causeway across swamps. If the enemy were to break through and block this causeway the Norfolks would be trapped and annihilated.

The morning hours crawled by as Jim Wright waited with the other drivers. At 1.30 p.m. they left their slit-trenches and stood by their vehicles ready to move off at the pre-arranged hour of two o'clock. Jim lit a cigarette to relieve his taut nerves, but it tasted rank and he stamped it out after a few puffs. He climbed up into the driving seat; even this small action seemed better than just standing about.

He had hardly settled himself before heavy firing of machine-guns and mortars broke out not far away. He grasped his rifle and leapt out of the vehicle into his slit-trench, peering anxiously into the surrounding undergrowth. Then an officer came running towards them, shouting:

'Get your trucks out on to the road quickly! Jap tanks are coming! Get moving!'

Without waiting to go out at the normal exit point which was some way off, Jim put his truck into low gear and drove hard across the ditch alongside the road, praying that he would not get stuck. He joined the others and they moved off at once, driving through smoke and flames, though Jim could not see what was burning. They cleared the causeway over the swamps and, passing through Yong Peng, drove into a rubber plantation just south of the town. Here he waited in comparative safety, thinking anxiously about his comrades who were even now fighting a desperate rear-guard battle out of the defile and along the causeway.

Before dusk word came through that they had been successful, had blown up several culverts to delay the Japanese tanks and were now marching the remaining seven miles back to Yong Peng. The survivors arrived soon after midnight and Jim helped them into his truck. Among them was Bert Hall, an old friend from Sheringham, but many familiar faces were missing.

The Norfolks moved at once to a plantation well south of Ayer Hitam where they enjoyed a few hours' sleep, their first for several days. Only a week had passed since they had driven north from Singapore; it had seemed a lifetime and in that short period the effective strength of the battalion had been reduced to twenty-two officers and 483 men. However, it could have been much worse; the Japanese had failed to trap them in the defile or to capture the vital Yong Peng road junction.

Their relief, however, was to be short-lived.

CHAPTER TWO

The Water Tower and After

Jim Wright left Ayer Hitam soon after midnight on 24 January. As he drove south to Skudai before turning west to the coast, his exhausted passengers slept in the back of the lorry. It was still dark when he reached Pontian Kechil and followed the road north to Benut, Rengit and Senggarang. Arriving at Senggarang soon after dawn, he dropped the men in his lorry and set off back to B Echelon with orders to collect and bring forward another party the following day.

Having had no hot food for several days and little apart from a few dry biscuits, he was very hungry and decided to stop and look for a fallen coconut in one of the many plantations along the road. At last he saw a promising spot and brought his lorry to a halt. He was half out of his seat when, to his amazement, a light machine-gun opened fire on him. He had scrambled back into his cab and started the engine when the lorry which had been behind him, and which had also stopped, tore past him, the driver shouting something which he could not hear. He noticed that there were bullet holes in the near-side of the other vehicle.

Jim lost no time in getting away and was soon speeding down the road. That night, 25 January, he spent at B Echelon which was well back near Skudai, and there at last he had a hot meal and a good wash. He inspected his lorry and found that it had been riddled with bullets; he thanked his lucky stars for having come through the ambush unscathed. Then he climbed into an open truck with the other three drivers and they lay close to each other in order to keep warm while they slept.

There were now only four vehicles available for ferrying

reinforcements forward. Jim was horrified, in view of his experiences the previous day, to find that he had to do the trip again at dawn, escorted by one armoured car, the remaining three vehicles to follow on later in the morning.

At first light he followed the armoured car, in which was Brigadier Duke, commander of 53rd Infantry Brigade, out on to the road and headed north. They arrived at Rengit water tower without incident, but found a battle in progress there. The senior officer told Brigadier Duke that the road to Seng-garang was now blocked by strong enemy forces and that pressure on the Rengit positions was increasing. Duke told Jim to drop his passengers here, to destroy his vehicle and to join the men who were manning the defensive positions near the water tower.

The battle raged on, the Japanese using the water tower as a mark for their mortar fire while their infantry worked round the defenders' flanks. Jim, having put his lorry completely out of action, crouched behind one of the brick pillars supporting a house. There had been no time to dig a slit-trench and there was little cover from the bursting mortar bombs.

Hardly had he taken up his position than the other three reinforcement lorries, led by a carrier and with some armoured cars, passed through Rengit. Jim watched as they drove on towards the spot where he had been ambushed the day before. However, he had no time to worry about them now. The Japanese seemed to be everywhere and many hand-to-hand fights were taking place. Snipers hidden in trees were giving them a great deal of trouble so a man near Jim sprayed the trees with his Bren gun and one Japanese soldier fell to the ground.

Throughout the morning the Japanese continued to press home their attacks until it seemed inevitable that they would soon overrun A Company. Standing in the open on the road was a truck which had been riddled with bullets and shell splinters. CSM M. E. Rudling, who had in the past been sergeant of the Mortar Platoon, knew that it contained a three-inch mortar and some bombs. Calling Jim and two others to follow him, they crawled across the open ground to the truck, bullets whipping over their backs. They leapt in and grabbed the mortar and bombs and dashed back to their positions through a hail of fire which, by some miracle, left them unscathed. They set up the weapon and, as the Japanese were very close, had to fire the bombs almost vertically into the air. The effect on the Japanese was devastating and they quickly fell back as the bombs tore into them.

When the last one had been fired, Jim took up a position behind one of the concrete posts which held the chains surrounding the water tower. Enemy machine-gun fire often struck the tower and its supports, bringing down clouds of choking concrete dust. Jim's water bottle had long since been emptied and the dust increased his raging thirst.

Suddenly an officer whose name Jim did not know charged forward to the edge of the undergrowth and, right under the noses of the Japanese, snatched up a wounded British soldier. Slinging the man over his shoulder, he dashed back under heavy fire. Jim did not see if he reached safety with his burden but was filled with admiration for his courageous act.

However, he had little time to dwell on it. The Japanese suddenly surged in on his right and almost overran them before being driven back by heavy fire, leaving several of their dead on the ground.

During the afternoon Lieutenant Mackwood, who had been with the convoy which had passed through Rengit during the morning, arrived back at the water tower in a very shaken state. He reported that the convoy had run into a strong enemy road block between Rengit and Senggarang and, before anyone could get out of the trucks, they had been subjected to intense machine-gun fire. He himself had been lucky as he had been in the armoured car at the rear of the convoy and his driver had managed to back the vehicle out of the shambles until he was able to turn and get back to Rengit. Mackwood said that he had seen no other survivors and thought that virtually the whole force had been wiped out instantly, most of them still in the trucks. This proved true: only two officers and a few men eventually made their way to safety on foot.

Under the pitiless afternoon sun the weary and parched defenders kept the Japanese at bay, but casualties were mounting steadily. By dusk the survivors were concentrated round the tower and it was obvious that the position could not be held for much longer. The enemy had now encircled them and had cut the road back to Brigade HQ at Benut which lay about ten miles to the south-east. Brigadier Duke therefore gave orders that Rengit was to be abandoned during the early hours of 27

January and that the defenders must make their way on foot to new positions at Benut. As all vehicles had been destroyed, the road-blocks were now irrelevant, but the problem of carrying out the badly wounded was acute.

Lieutenant Calder, now commanding this remnant of A Company, skilfully disengaged from the battle by first going north and crossing the road. Turning south-east he then worked his way in the darkness through the rubber and coconut plantations, reaching Benut the following day.

CSM Rudling, who, with CSM Kelf of the depleted C Company, was acting as rearguard at the water tower during the Company's withdrawal, found himself in a perilous situation as the Japanese were again creeping forward and snipers were firing at the two men at very close range in the moonlight. Finally, when a bullet had torn off the rim of Kelf's steel helmet, they decided that it was time to follow the others. Jumping to their feet they dashed across the road and into some bushes where the snipers could not see them.

But they had left it too late. In the darkness and thick foliage they became separated. As Kelf had been carrying the Bren gun, Rudling was now unarmed. With the Japanese so close he dared not call out to Kelf (who eventually caught up with the Company) but continued to move quietly through the undergrowth until he reached a small party of lost men, several of whom were wounded. Two of them had leg wounds and were being carried by their companions.

With this party was Jim Wright. In the darkness and noise of battle near the water tower he, and a few men near him, had suddenly become aware that they were totally isolated. They could hear the Japanese moving in the bushes around them and realized that they could not stay there any longer. They had no idea in which direction their comrades had gone, but, with their casualties, they managed to dash across the road and into some thick bushes. Then they walked quietly north for a hundred yards or so until they reached some deserted Chinese shacks. Here they turned west along a path which ran through swamps until they were well clear of the road.

While they debated in whispers what to do next, CSM Rudling appeared. Taking charge, he decided to carry the two wounded to the coast, which was between one and two miles away, in the hope of finding a small boat in which they could be

ferried south. Rudling had no map or compass but followed the
water-courses which he guessed ran from Rengit to the sea. It
was hard going; the men were exhausted and those carrying the
wounded collapsed on several occasions but, in spite of this, no
one complained or thought of abandoning them.

At last they came to a creek beside which they lit a fire and
boiled enough water to fill their water bottles; as they had had
neither food nor drink during the past twenty-four hours they
were all becoming very dehydrated. It appeared that they
would have to cross the creek which, although shallow, had
very steep banks up and down which it would have been
impossible to carry the wounded. With their bayonets they cut
strong saplings and made rough stretchers on which they were
able to drag them across.

By now it was daylight and they had come to the mangrove
swamps which fringe so much of this coast. Rudling sent two
men to look for a boat and, before very long, they spotted a
small native canoe off the mouth of the river. They called out to
the occupants who brought the boat in to the shore. They
turned out to be two men of the 5th Norfolks who had made for
the coast when the Senggarang positions had been abandoned
thirty-six hours previously. They had been lucky enough to find
this frail craft. It would hold four at a pinch so they agreed to
take the two wounded men and, when they had been put on
board, they set off again down the coast towards Singapore.
Whether they reached safety or suffered the same fate as so
many of their comrades is not known.

Rudling's party, relieved of the burden of the two casualties,
then moved back towards the road between Rengit and Benut,
the right direction for Singapore as far as they could judge.
They had to cross two rivers which ran down to the sea, and this
they did with the help of ropes which some Royal Engineers
with the party rigged across the water. During their journey
they met another group of men heading for Singapore, but these
decided not to join up with them.

This meeting was typical of what was happening all over
Johore. Everywhere there were small parties of men who had
been cut off and were trying to get back to our own forces. They
were usually without officers, maps* or compasses, food or

* A train loaded with maps had been lost to the Japanese further north. Junior
leaders, newly-arrived in Malaya, had to fight without benefit of maps.

medical supplies, and had only a vague idea of where they were going. Meanwhile the Japanese hunted them down ruthlessly, aided by Indian and Malay informers, and many of these parties never reached safety.

Rudling realized that it was imperative to re-cross the Rengit–Benut road and to move parallel to it on the east side. Where they were now there was little room for manoeuvre, if the Japanese were to attack them, in the narrow strip between the road and the sea. Furthermore, much of this strip of land was inhabited, so there was always the chance that they might be betrayed and ambushed.

Presently they came to a Malay *kampong* where the villagers produced a four-gallon can of weak tea. While they were drinking this, a good deal of argument arose about which way they should go next. Jim Wright had teamed up with a friend, Private R. Marler from Norwich, who now said:

'We're not getting anywhere. Let's go off on our own.'

Jim agreed and Marler gave him two clips of ammunition as they were both very short after the fighting at Rengit water tower. They slipped away from Rudling's party* and, after travelling a few miles, took shelter in a small shack for the night. They started out again at dawn and soon came to a *kampong* where they met another party of soldiers whom they joined. Before they reached the road they heard sounds of heavy fire from the direction of Benut. Some of the men began to panic, and Marler suggested to Jim once more that they would do better by themselves.

'I think we ought to stick with the others,' Jim replied.

'Then give me back my bloody clips!' said Marler angrily, and, snatching them from Jim, he strode off alone. As it turned out, this was a very unwise decision: Marler was captured by the Japanese later that day and died of dysentery in Kuala Lumpur jail six weeks later.

Jim went on with the rest of the party. During the afternoon

---

* Rudling's party was ambushed that night as they tried to cross the road. His few remaining companions were killed during the following days. He travelled alone for two weeks towards Singapore, twice narrowly escaping capture after betrayal by Malays, once nearly drowning when swimming a river, finally killing a Japanese soldier with his bare hands. Starving and exhausted, he reached the Johore Straits but was captured and condemned to execution. He was later reprieved and taken to Changi after Singapore had fallen.

they arrived back at the road. While they were debating their next move a platoon of Japanese came along on bicycles and they had to dive for cover. Abandoning the idea of crossing in daylight they pushed on parallel to the road and soon picked up some more stragglers, mainly from Royal Artillery units. By now they were very tired, and almost out of drinking water again. They were close to the road and had to move very warily, making slow progress. As soon as darkness fell they decided to cross it. But only a few men had made the crossing when a party of Japanese appeared and attacked those still on the west side. In the ensuing fight there were many casualties and the British party was scattered.

Jim Wright was one of the few who had got across, and he hid himself quickly when he heard the shooting. But within minutes the Japanese attacked on his side of the road as well. At first they were beaten back but they soon rallied and came in again. In the darkness and confusion Jim suddenly realized that he was alone, his companions having moved off without his knowledge. Then he saw faint moonlight glinting on the bayonets of three or four Japanese quite close to him. He dodged away among the trees and kept going until he was well clear of the scene.

When daylight came on 29 January he was still alone, so he decided to get even further away from the road. During the morning he came upon a party of about twenty men whom he did not know, as they were a mixture from many units, and he joined them. They moved cautiously all day and during the night concealed themselves in thick country and tried to get some rest. Mosquitoes and hunger prevented any of them from doing more than doze fitfully and uncomfortably.

The next day they moved off again, mainly through rubber and coconut plantations. Here the tracks were good but there was a great risk that Japanese bicycle patrols might surprise them, so they kept under cover as much as possible.

Unfortunately, during the afternoon, this is just what did happen. The group ran into a strong enemy fighting patrol and was quickly surrounded. An officer went forward to the Japanese, waving a handkerchief, with a view to surrendering the party and avoiding further casualties. He talked with them for several minutes and the Japanese then called everyone forward to surrender. As the British advanced in a group, machine-guns opened up on them and within seconds there was a heap of bodies lying on the ground.

Amazingly, Jim's luck was still holding out. He was at the back of the party as it moved forward and at the first burst of fire he threw himself into a small dip in the ground. The noise was deafening but above the chatter of the machine-guns he could hear the cries of the wounded and dying. There were some bushes at the end of the dip and these hid him from the Japanese gunners. He inched his way backwards behind the bushes and by the time the firing had died down he had got himself into some thick reeds where he was well concealed, though very wet. It was quite quiet now and he could hear the Japanese talking excitedly over the bodies of his companions, only a few yards from where he lay. He dared not move further into the swamp for fear that rustling reeds would attract the enemy's attention. Eventually they went away and silence fell.

Just before dusk, Jim peered cautiously out of his hiding place. There seemed to be no living survivors of the massacre so he crawled further into the swamp where he spent a very uncomfortable night, half submerged in mud and water, tormented by myriads of mosquitoes and with his mind in a state of turmoil. He was so frightened by what he had seen that he hardly noticed his physical discomforts. He now had no doubts about his fate if the enemy should catch him. It was at this point he determined that he would never surrender; better to be killed fighting than just to be slaughtered in cold blood.

At dawn he crawled further into the swamp just in case the Japanese chose to return to the scene. He kept going slowly, sometimes up to his waist in water and slime, until at last he reached some firmer ground where he could move more easily. During the afternoon he came to a Malay *kampong* where he met two other soldiers. More joined them until there were about sixteen in all, some of them from the 6th Norfolks, and Jim was delighted to be reunited with friends. He fervently hoped that he would not find himself alone ever again.

But the Malays in the village were hostile, refusing to help the soldiers in any way or to sell them food. When night fell they bolted their doors and the men slept on the open verandahs, plagued as usual by mosquitoes. At first light they set off again towards Singapore and for two hours struggled through *bĕlukar* (thick secondary jungle). At last they reached a good track and soon came to a Malay shop. The owner wore bandages and, as far as they could gather, had been knocked about by a visiting Japanese patrol. He was unfriendly, but grudgingly sold them some food and was obviously relieved when they moved on.

During the afternoon they noticed some military signal cables lying along the edge of the track. Some signallers with the party confirmed that they were of British origin so they followed them in the hope of finding some other British troops. Jim was walking at the tail of the party. As he passed a small house a man came out and made signs that he wished to speak to him. Jim hesitated and went back a few yards, then changed his mind and hurried on after his companions. He could not bear the thought of being alone again if he stopped to chat and lost sight of them.

Hardly had he caught up with the others than they ran into a Japanese ambush. Fire was heavy and there were several casualties but they returned the fire and attacked the enemy, trying to break out of the trap into which they had fallen. Jim felt a blow on his right foot which then went completely numb. His rifle had been shot out of his hand and lay splintered beside him; his steel helmet had also been hit and knocked off his head.

In the confusion it flashed through his mind that the man he had seen had been trying to warn him of this ambush, and he wished with all his heart that he had stopped to talk to him. With two others he sprinted towards some bushes, bullets flying all about them and his companions falling dead before they reached cover. Jim had lost all feeling in his right foot; he did not know whether it was on the ground or not and he stumbled and fell as he ran. Perhaps this made him a difficult target. Whatever the reason, he was not hit and managed to get into some *bělukar*, where he found five others who had escaped the ambush. They all pressed further into the thick cover and, as it was now dusk, the Japanese did not follow them.

After a while they stopped to rest and to take stock of their situation. Jim had been hit in the foot by an explosive bullet which had blown off the side of his boot and made a large wound. Two of the other five had also been wounded, but were able to walk. His companions helped Jim to bandage his foot and then they all tried to get some sleep. Jim found this impossible as the feeling returned to his foot and he was in intense pain.

Their position was not an enviable one: six men, three of whom were wounded, exhausted and frightened by the ordeals through which they had recently passed, without a leader, map or compass, and having little idea where they were or in which direction to go. Their chances of survival were small – and they knew it.

At dawn on 2 February they moved slowly on through the thick undergrowth. Jim's foot had now stiffened and it was agony to put it to the ground. At first he was helped by a man on either side of him, but later, as they became exhausted by their efforts and the other wounded needed attention, Jim had only one man to help him. Gradually they both became enfeebled and fell further and further behind the others.

Suddenly, without saying anything, Jim's companion lowered him to the ground and hurried on after the rest of the party. At first he was astonished but then, realizing that his helper was not coming back, Jim watched in silence until the man disappeared from sight. He felt no fear or emotion at that moment, just physically exhausted and utterly miserable. Then it dawned on him that it would soon be dark; the thought of spending a night, alone and helpless, in the dank jungle filled him with dread. But he could not, and still cannot find it in his heart to criticize the man who left him there. It was a desperate choice.

CHAPTER THREE

The Ordeal Begins

That first night alone was a very long one. As dawn came Jim was roused by the shrill cries of some small birds. Half-awake, he automatically stretched out a hand for his rifle and then, finding nothing, remembered the ambush and the events which followed. He tried to muster his failing energies and decide what he should do. The first thing was to get out of the jungle and find water and food; the second was to get some treatment for his shattered foot.

Spurred on by these imperatives he started to crawl towards the rising sun; he remembered that he and his companions had been travelling south-east before the Japanese ambushed them. Crawling was painful because his injured foot trailed and bumped on the ground with each movement. Unable to bear this after a while, he turned round into a sitting position and, holding his foot off the ground, edged slowly forward, taking his weight on his hands, seat and left foot.

But this way of proceeding was exhausting and he had to have frequent rests. It seemed to take hours to cover a few hundred yards. By now the sun was high in the sky and, although he was in shade in the jungle, the steaming, enervating heat increased his thirst and fatigue. Food had ceased to have much importance compared to his need for water.

Throughout the day he crabbed painfully ahead but, by the time darkness fell, he had found no water nor had he come to the edge of the jungle. Physically the day had drained him of his last reserves and, as he crawled to a tree and propped himself against it, he knew that he was nearly finished. Here, mercifully, he slept, unconscious of his wound or of his thirst or even of the tormenting swarms of mosquitoes.

It was still dark when he woke, shivering because a heavy dew had fallen during the night and his clothes were soaking. He sat shaking with cold while the jungle reverberated with noises which set his nerves on edge. Never had the dawn been so welcome. Gritting his teeth he started to slither forward again.

At last, soon after noon, he came to the jungle edge and before long found a path. Here the dense thickets of *bĕlukar* gave way to heavily wooded country in which clumps of bamboo and other bushes were interspersed with open glades. It seemed likely that the path would lead him to a plantation or a village, but he realized that he would simply have to get up on his feet and walk.

He hobbled painfully along until he came to some huts. He approached cautiously, but found them deserted. By one of the huts was a cooking fire but the ashes were cold. Limping on, he suddenly froze as he saw a movement ahead. An old Chinese man was digging his garden. He had not seen Jim, and, after making sure that no one else was in sight, Jim went closer and called to him in a low voice.

Startled, the man looked up. Seeing that Jim was in trouble, he helped him into his house and gave him some water and biscuits. He also produced a stout stick to help him on his way. Mumbling in Chinese and making signs, he managed to convey the message that Japanese patrols were everywhere and often bicycled along this very path. He also warned Jim to avoid Malays and Indians as they would betray him if they could.

Jim tested the stick but found that it sank into the ground as he had to put so much weight on it in order to save his foot. Seeing this, the old man took it and quickly nailed a flat piece of wood across the bottom, which solved the problem.

In view of the old man's warning, Jim left the footpath and kept to the bushes which bordered it. Presently he came to some empty shacks and stopped to rest on a verandah. While he was there, a group of Malays arrived and came to look at him. They talked excitedly among themselves, then jeered at him and ran off.

Fearing that they had gone to tell the Japanese about him, he left the place as quickly as he could and plunged on through the bushes until he reckoned that he had thrown them off the scent. He then stopped for a rest and tried to do something about the bandage on his foot. But it was hopeless; the dressing had become little more than a filthy piece of twisted rag. He noticed that his foot was now beginning to smell horribly, as if it was already septic.

He hobbled on until he came to another path crossing his. Some sixth sense warned him to be extra careful, and sure enough there was a Japanese patrol, a bare hundred yards away and coming straight towards him. He scrambled desperately into a thicket of *mengkuang* and waited, hardly daring to breathe.

But they had not seen or heard him and soon passed by, carelessly chatting to each other. It struck Jim that, ironically, perhaps the only true thing which he had been told about the Japanese was that many of them had very poor eyesight.

When they had gone he had some difficulty in getting out of his prickly refuge. By now it was evening and he knew that he must find a safe spot in which to spend the night. He moved away from the track until he was certain that he could not be seen or heard by anyone passing along it. As he lowered himself to the ground at the foot of a large tree it started to rain, and he was soon soaked and cold. Worse still were the *kerengga* (red ants), to whom the tree evidently belonged and which stung him frequently in the darkness. The jungle noises seemed louder than ever and he felt thoroughly scared after his brush with the Japanese patrol, so it was hardly surprising that he did not sleep much.

The following morning his foot was so painful that he made very little progress. He met no one, had nothing to eat or drink all day and settled down in the evening for another restless night. At first light he struggled up again and went on, following the edge of the track which was well-used and had on it some fresh footmarks. Coming round a bend he met three Malay boys who asked for a light for their cigarettes. When he made signs that he had no matches they laughed at him and ran off.

Later Jim came to a pineapple plantation. He went into it and cut off a fruit with his bayonet, the only piece of equipment he had managed to keep. But the pineapple was green and sour inside, so he threw it away.

Skirting a *kampong*, he came out of the bushes to a house which turned out to be a Chinese laundry. The owners were friendly but seconds after his arrival an alarm was given and he was hustled behind some piles of dirty washing. A Japanese patrol appeared and wandered round the building but did not spot him. As soon as they had gone the Chinese, now very frightened, gave him some rice and water and made signs that he should go away at once.

He pushed on, but by now he was extremely tired and was having to rest more and more frequently. Presently he came upon a party of Malays who were washing clothes in a small watercourse. Their chatter died as they turned and stared at him in silence. After a pause two men came forward and gave him some water, but another, who was obviously a headman, sent them to fetch coffee. Jim drank this gratefully, but as these were the first Malays who had helped him, he felt uneasy, and after thanking the headman he continued on his painful journey.

He was limping badly by the time he came to another Chinese house. The owner quickly helped him up into a loft where he covered him with empty rice bags. The man must have had good hearing because, within a minute or two, a Japanese patrol visited the house and searched it. At last they went away and the Chinese came up to the loft with food and water. While Jim was enjoying this some Japanese planes flew over and the man shook his fist at them. When Jim had had enough to eat his host helped him down and went with him to the edge of the track. Suddenly he pushed Jim down into a ditch as a lorry full of Japanese swept past, luckily without seeing him.

He kept to the shelter of a rubber plantation and soon came to another Chinese *kampong*. Here the occupants were less welcoming, telling him that the Japanese had taken away all their women and that they were very frightened. They begged him to go away, saying that the Japanese would kill them all if they were to find him near their houses. It was now nearly dusk so he moved on for half a mile and then concealed himself in some cover for the night.

It had been a good day because he had had some food, water and coffee, but he realized that he could not hope to escape the notice of the Japanese if he stayed in this inhabited area.

However, he slept better than he had done since he had been wounded.

The rise in his spirits had reduced his alertness and the next morning he was foolishly walking along the path when he heard the sound of an engine. As he leapt into the bushes alongside the track a lorry-load of Japanese, all dressed in white singlets, came round a corner ahead of him. The vehicle stopped and they all jumped to the ground. He was certain that they had seen him and, despite the pain in his foot, he tried to run further into the undergrowth. Suddenly he pitched head first into a ditch, full of water and overhung by trees and long grass. As quietly as possible he crawled along it for a short distance before lying quite still, almost submerged.

He had had such a fright that he stayed in the ditch long after he heard the lorry drive away. Dripping with mud and water, he crawled cautiously out and listened. Everything was quiet so he moved on slowly, keeping to the cover beside the path. Before long he met an old Chinese man who told him that the Japanese had been looting the *kampong*. He boiled Jim an egg and gave him cigarettes, matches and bananas. Jim asked him for a hat and he produced a smart white topee. When Jim said that this would be too conspicuous, he gave him an old trilby which was much more suitable. He then drew a map on a piece of paper to show him how to get to Singapore and kept saying that he must go via Lee's pineapple factory. Then he wished Jim luck and put him on his road.

After a time Jim came to a Chinese *kampong* in a rubber plantation; some of the inhabitants were sitting outside having haircuts, but they were so nervous that they refused to look at him or talk to him, and some of them rushed into their houses and bolted their doors. He went on until he found some thick cover and again hid himself for the night.

The following afternoon, as he was pushing his way through tall sharp grass, called *lalang*, dogs began to bark. He stopped and crouched down, but the barking became louder. Then a Chinese man, carrying a bicycle, pushed through the grass and saw Jim. Bidding his dogs to be quiet, he muttered 'Japun!' and motioned to him to keep down and stay still. Jim needed no second bidding and lay flat as the man walked on.

He waited, worried because it was getting late and he had yet to find a safe place for the night, but he dared not come out of hiding until he was certain that the Japanese had gone. At last all seemed quiet and he went on for a little until he found a swamp which gave him good cover.

By now he was mentally and physically drained. Although during the past two days he had been getting more food and drink than hitherto, it had been gained at a terrible risk of capture. So far he had been lucky in meeting mainly Chinese, many of whom had helped him, but he could not expect such luck to last indefinitely. His many escapes preyed on his mind and added to his tiredness; in addition, the pain in his foot seemed to be increasing. With these thoughts he fell into an uneasy sleep for a few hours.

Starting out again at dawn he soon came to a broad and deep river, probably the upper reaches of the Sungei Benut. This was a serious obstacle; apart from his exhaustion and injury, he could not swim. Also he had heard that the rivers of Malaya were infested with crocodiles. (In fact, by 1942 crocodiles were not common, but there were still a few, and Jim was quite right to fear them.)

He walked along the bank until he came to a fallen tree which almost bridged the river. As he was getting down the bank he heard voices and sank into the water, holding on to a branch. Two Japanese carrying rifles walked along the bank just above him but did not see him.

He remained motionless until they had disappeared from view and then waded out into the river alongside the tree trunk. He was soon out of his depth and had to move hand over hand along the branches. When he reached the last branch, he lowered his feet slowly and found that he could stand on the bottom, so he struggled ashore and found somewhere to lie up for the night.

Crossing the river seemed to have taken him away from the villages and for the next two days he hobbled on, mainly through rubber plantations, without seeing a soul. Water was less of a problem but he did not have any food and by nightfall each day he was dead beat, yet unable to sleep soundly.

It was becoming clear to him that his fatigue was accumulating and was preventing him from sleeping; as well as the pain of his foot, every muscle in his body ached. Singapore, as far as he had been able to gather from the Chinese, was about fifty miles away, and he realized that, at his present rate of progress, the journey might take weeks. In the very near future he would have to find some place where he could stop for a few days and recuperate, otherwise he would soon be too exhausted to move. Each dawn came as a challenge and it required increased effort and determination to get under way.

His route now was mostly through rubber, but once he had a difficult time getting through an oil palm plantation in which was a thick knee-high growth of prickly bushes. He saw few paths and avoided them for fear of meeting Japanese patrols. Gradually, he found his way taking him downhill, which eased his legs. He kept stopping and listening and watching, and then moving on again. For two more days he saw no one and began to get very hungry.

On the afternoon of the second day he came to a Chinese hut and approached it warily. The owners were very frightened when they saw him as the Japanese had recently surrounded the house and had cut the throats of some of them, for no obvious reason. They had little food, but they hurriedly gave him three raw sweet potatoes and sent him away.

By now he could hear the noise of vehicles quite regularly and he felt sure he was coming to a road. An hour after leaving the Chinese hut, he reached it and crept into some thick cover at the edge where he sat listening and watching. There was an almost continuous flow of military traffic, much of it consisting of captured British trucks. Jim saw that it was far too dangerous to cross the road in daylight so he crawled behind a fallen tree a little way back from the roadside and had a smoke.

While sitting there he noticed, on the other side of the road, a milestone, and he strained his eyes to read what it said – Singapore 40 Ayer Hitam 18. So this was the very road along which he had driven in convoy to Yong Peng, perhaps in one of these same trucks. Was it really only four weeks ago? The difference in his circumstances then and now filled him with a wave of misery.

CHAPTER FOUR

Journey out of Nightmare

With the coming of night, the traffic was reduced to some extent and Jim decided to cross the road during a lull. As he crept down to the edge he ran into some barbed wire which he had not noticed in daylight. He was in the open here and hurriedly forced his way through it, tearing his clothes and scratching himself badly. At the edge he stood still and listened; he could hear no traffic, so he hobbled across the road as quickly as he could. After his weeks in the jungle he felt terribly naked and exposed out on the broad highway.

Hardly had he gained the shelter of some rubber trees on the other side than a convoy of trucks roared past, their headlights stabbing the darkness. Jim crouched, motionless, until they had gone and then moved further into the rubber where he propped himself against a tree and tried to get some rest.

He was too close to the road for safety so, just before dawn, he started out again. His foot was even more stiff and painful than usual and seemed very swollen. He had to get some treatment for it as soon as possible.

He met one Chinese but the man ran away before he could speak to him. Soon afterwards he came to a solitary house where an Indian was preparing his morning meal. Wary because of the warnings the Chinese had given him about Malays and Indians who betrayed British soldiers to the Japanese, he remained hidden for a while and watched the man. As the Indian appeared to be alone Jim decided to risk it, especially as the smell of the cooking was blowing his way and making his mouth water.

After his initial surprise the Indian was very friendly; it

seemed almost as if he was used to having wounded soldiers drop in on him for breakfast. He gave Jim a hot *chapatti* which he ate hungrily. In good English he warned him to be on the alert as Japanese patrols often passed by his house. He added that he felt sorry for him; many Indian soldiers who had been cut off had just put on civilian clothes and melted into the background in Indian communities but of course this was not possible for a white man.

Jim thanked him for the food and, heeding his warning, left the track. Eventually he found himself in a swamp where he felt safer, but where his progress was very slow and exhausting. Wallowing on, sometimes up to his waist in the slime and frequently becoming bogged down, at last he could go no further. Finding a slightly drier place, he settled down for the night. At least he had a little food inside him and there was no shortage of water, however unpalatable it might look. But his foot was agony after his struggles in the mud, and mosquitoes and leeches swarmed on him mercilessly.

The next morning he was still so tired that he decided to stay all that day and the following night in the swamp. While he rested he tried to plan what he should do. Singapore was his destination; he felt that he must get there if he was to survive. But it was still forty miles away by road and he could not risk using the road, even by night. On his journey, since he had been wounded, he had covered about fifteen miles, as far as he could judge, and it had taken him about two weeks. At that rate of progress Singapore was six weeks' travelling away; he knew that he would never make it. Apart from the increased chances of betrayal and capture as he approached the more populous country near Johore Bahru, he was utterly worn out and had lost a lot of weight and strength. He had tried to clean up his foot but it bled continuously and, in the swamp, was always covered with leeches. It smelt abominably and he was unable to protect it with the wisp of material which had started as a bandage two weeks earlier.

With these depressing thoughts in mind he struggled on through the swamp at daybreak next morning. Before long he came to dry ground and out on to a path. He followed this for a short distance and came to some houses. They were deserted, but there were pigs and chickens running about. He wondered where the owners were. As he came to a wider track, the absence of people suddenly filled him with fear and suspicion.

Leaving the path at once he climbed painfully up a hill beside it, pushing his way through the *lalang*. At last he reached the top which was clear of trees and from here he could see quite a distance. Away to the north was a large village on a railway line* and down in a valley just below him were seven small houses. He watched them for some time. As far as he could tell they seemed to be occupied by Chinese, so he decided to visit them.

It was now almost dusk and, exhausted by his climb up the hill, he settled down for the night, feeling comparatively safe.

At dawn he came down and moved silently towards the houses. When he was near he stopped and watched them for a few minutes. He decided to ask the Chinese occupants for help. As he approached they saw him and seemed very nervous. They made him go behind one of the houses and hide while they prepared some food for him.

When Jim had eaten, a very smart Chinese man was brought to see him. He spoke excellent English and said that he had been a shopkeeper in Johore Bahru. He had come to this *kampong* to get away from the Japanese, but they had searched the houses and taken his wife away. He had been out every day looking for her but had been unable to find any trace of her. The house belonged to his father and he had brought his wife and two small sons of seven and eight, both of whom spoke English, to live there until things quietened down a bit in Johore Bahru. He told Jim that Singapore had fallen on 15 February and that it was no use him trying to get there now. He advised him to hide in the jungle and wait until the British returned, which, he said, would not be long.

He and his sons were very kind to Jim, giving him as much food as he wanted, and it was a joy to be able to speak to someone who could understand him. But the news of the fall of Singapore was a shattering blow and he now had to think of a new plan for the future. Like the Chinese, he felt sure that the British would soon invade Malaya and recapture it; all he had to do was hold on until they came. He feared the Japanese for their ruthless atrocities, but he was also beginning to feel some contempt for them. They had been so short-sighted and inept on the many occasions on which he had run into them that he

* This was Layang Layang

could not see them beating well-trained and well-armed British soldiers. And they were so hideous and bandy-legged that he could not help feeling far superior to them.

But they were also dangerous and very cruel; and they were the masters of Malaya now. The Chinese were terrified of them. The Chinese shopkeeper told Jim that they had made a speciality of killing and torturing the Chinese, surrounding the villages, beheading the men and torturing the women after raping them, often cutting off their breasts. All this was undoubtedly part of a policy of terrorizing any opposition, but the Japanese were sufficiently degraded and sadistic to enjoy these orgies of murder and torture. He said that all the young people had left the villages and were hiding in the jungle so that they could not be surprised by Japanese attacks. Only the old people were left in the villages to look after the houses and livestock, and to buy food and cook it for those in hiding. Sometimes the Japanese killed the old people and sometimes they didn't; these ancients lived on a knife-edge, with resignation and a fatalistic acceptance of their possible lot.

After this conversation and a meal, they took Jim away from the house and up a hill covered with small rubber trees and pineapples. They said that there was a hut in the jungle in which he could stay. After pointing it out, the Chinese went back to their house and Jim went on to meet the Chinese man who owned the hut. He explained with signs that he wanted to sleep there, and at last the man understood and nodded his head. There was a bed raised on poles off the ground and, when the owner had gone, Jim lay on this and rested his foot. He tried to sleep but mosquitoes tormented him all night and he felt very cold. His foot was a worry. It was now so painful that he could hardly put it on the ground.

After a miserable night he crawled out of the hut and down the hill towards the houses. His Chinese friend met him and said that he must not come any nearer as it was far too dangerous for all of them. He promised to bring food halfway up the hill just before dusk every evening. He gave Jim some rice balls and small pieces of pork. These were delicious but there was not enough of it and he still felt very hungry. Some Chinese boys came up to the hut later and Jim gave them some money and asked them to get him something to eat. They went away and came back with some rice and an old kettle. He lit a

fire and tried to cook the rice but he did not know how to do it
and put in too much, ending with a solid inedible lump.

He slept that night in the hut, again made miserable by the
mosquitoes and the cold. At dawn he woke shivering and,
feeling something against his head, rose on his elbow to see
what it was. To his horror he saw a huge snake which had coiled
up by his head while he slept. At his movement it slithered away
and disappeared into the undergrowth. The incident gave Jim a
real fright; he hated snakes and this one had been too big and
too close for comfort. He lay resting in the hut all day, recover-
ing from the shock.

Time dragged by. At last a Chinese arrived with the food and
Jim asked if he could have something with which to cover
himself at night, to keep out the cold and the mosquitoes. The
man went away and later came back with a rice sack, saying
that it was all he could find. Jim got into it and it came up to his
waist, but the mosquitoes managed to get into it too, and it was
not much help in keeping him warm. He spent another
wretched night shivering and slapping at the mosquitoes, but at
least he was not visited again by the snake.

He found the long days and nights in this hut very lonely and
irksome. He had plenty of time to think and, now that his dream
of getting to Singapore one day had evaporated, he could find
nothing much to put in its place. He drew strength from
thinking about his home and family. Because he was the
youngest of ten children and had been born soon after his eldest
brother had been killed on the Western Front in the Great War,
his relationship with his father and mother was especially close.
The thought of the effect his death would have on them was
unbearable and fortified his determination to get through this
ordeal somehow and to return home safely. To an outside
observer it would have presented an ironic picture – this
emaciated scarecrow, clad in a few rags and stinking from his
rotten foot, lying there and consoling himself with plans for his
homecoming.

Perhaps the hardest thing to bear was the fact that his only
safety lay in solitude. He yearned for company, someone to
whom he could talk, or just to see people walking about even if
he could not talk to them. He decided that he would move about
a bit more the next day and get closer to the houses so that he
could at least watch those who lived there.

As soon as the sun was up he took his rice sack and went part of the way down the hill. He found a place which overlooked the houses and lay down in the long grass. Presently a Chinese came walking up and almost stumbled over him. The man signed to him to keep down and stood looking across the valley, shading his eyes with one hand. He seemed quite calm, but it was obvious that something was going on over there which he did not like. Eventually he told Jim to return to the hut and went back down the hill.

The next morning Jim unwisely took up the same position overlooking the valley and was seen by some Indians. Soon after they had gone away he saw figures running about down below and they looked suspiciously like Japanese. He crawled into some thick thorny undergrowth and lay there with his rice sack. Before long he heard the chatter of voices and caught glimpses of some Japanese soldiers. They were searching for him, and at times they prodded into the bushes with their bayonets no more than two feet from where he lay. He gripped the hilt of his bayonet, determined to fight to the last if they found him.

After what seemed a lifetime, the Japanese moved further away until he could hear them no longer. He dared not go back to the hut, but at dusk he came out of the thicket and watched for any movement below. Presently the shopkeeper's two small sons came up to find him and told him that he had been betrayed to the Japanese by some Indians and that he must move on at once as they would be certain to return next day and make a more thorough search for him. The boys said that guides would take him to an area in which they knew that some other English soldiers were hiding, but he would have to search the jungle until he found them.

They took him down to the house and gave him a good meal of rice and a boiled egg. There were five Chinese standing by to take him on his journey. They had a four-gallon can of rice, cooking pots and matches, which they slung on poles between them. They all carried stout clubs with which to beat off any attempt by hostile natives to capture Jim and hand him over to the Japanese.

When he had eaten they set off and soon got on to the broad track which he had seen just before his arrival at the *kampong*. They walked on all night, passing through several Malay villages, but although Jim could just see them chatting and smoking outside their huts, no one spoke to them. The Chinese seemed very sure of themselves and of their destination, and Jim gathered that they felt safe at night on the country paths as the Japanese seldom went out during the hours of darkness, except in large numbers to carry out a dawn raid on some *kampong*.

In spite of the rest he had had over the past few days, Jim's foot was very painful, and the Chinese walked quite quickly. His privations were also catching up with him and soon after midnight he found that he was becoming lightheaded.

Just before dawn they crossed a small road and went up a track into the jungle. Along the track they came to a big house where Jim noticed a mongol boy, with a vastly swollen head, in a cage attached to the side of the house. Then they left the track and plunged into what seemed to Jim almost impenetrable jungle, but the Chinese appeared to know the way. It was very hard going for Jim and he was in a great deal of pain. Early in the morning they reached an *atap* hut. It was deserted; all the Chinese in the area had fled from the Japanese who now seldom came this way. The men shook hands with Jim and wished him luck. He watched them go and then, utterly worn out, he tottered to the hut's sleeping platform and fell asleep almost at once.

When he woke up it was already dark so he dared not light a fire to cook some rice. The night noises of the jungle were very loud here; every kind of animal and bird appeared to be coughing or squawking or rustling or crashing about. Jim had become used to fairly quiet nights in the cultivated country where he had been recently and his feelings of loneliness and fear increased. He sat out the night and waited for the sun to come up.

When it was light he surveyed his position. The hut stood at the foot of a steep cliff and was well camouflaged by palm fronds; a safe place if attacked, he thought, and almost invisible to anyone passing by.

But it was his first time in deep jungle and it filled him with dread. He was appalled at the prospect of trying to find the other soldiers in this gloomy tangle of vegetation. A thick carpet of dead leaves covered the ground and from it sprang millions of saplings which, in places, formed dense thickets over twelve feet high. Enormous tree trunks soared away above him until they were lost in a thick canopy of foliage which shut out all sunlight and dripped water continuously. Some of the trees were festooned with a tangled mass of creepers which hung down to the ground where they rooted again and climbed up adjacent trees. The sunless air hummed with insects and stank of rotting vegetation.

There was a stream about fifty yards away so Jim filled a pot and tried again to cook some rice. Unfortunately, as the Chinese had not taught him how to cook it, his efforts were hardly more successful than his first attempt had been, and he found the half-cooked rice nauseating. After he had eaten a little he boiled up some more water to drink and to bathe his foot. Both the bandage and his sock were by now tattered and evil-smelling and his boot was beginning to disintegrate. He lay about all day, feeling very depressed and wondering how on earth he was going to find the other British soldiers.

He was too disheartened by his failure with the rice to try cooking again that evening and lay awake in the darkness while the jungle throbbed with noise. Suddenly he heard a rustling and, in the faint moonlight, was just able to see that his shack had been invaded by several enormous rats, almost as big as cats. Alarmed, he kept them at bay with his stick until at last dawn came and they departed. No doubt they had been attracted by the smell of rice. Jim decided that he did not want to spend another night with them.

In the morning he had a look round and found a path which he followed. He kept hearing mournful cries and moved very warily. At last he saw that it was monkeys making the noise and there was no need to be afraid.

The path led eventually to a very make-shift shack where there were several Chinese men, women and children, with some dogs and chickens. Jim was amused to see, hanging up in the hut, smart suits, hats and suitcases. These were obviously well-to-do people who had fled from the Japanese. Jim asked them if he could sleep in a small hut nearby, and they said he could. They pointed to the chickens and said he could have one to eat, but he was too tired to bother and was soon asleep.

When he woke up next morning, apart from the jungle dawn chorus it seemed very quiet, and he found that the Chinese had fled during the night. He went on along the path and found another hut in which were two more Chinese. He told them he would come back the next day bringing the rice from his hut by the cliff, and he retraced his steps to it. In the morning, carrying the rice, he returned, but the Chinese had gone.

He walked on, hoping to find some trace of the British soldiers. By evening he realized that he was utterly lost and could not find the huts again nor any place which he could recognize. He spent a miserable night in the open and rain poured down on him until he was shaking with cold.

The next four days and nights were a nightmare. As he wandered in the jungle, completely lost and soaked by frequent downpours of rain, his strength began to ebb and, for the first time, he felt utterly defeated and began to fear that he would die.

He found no huts nor did he meet a living soul. Only the monkeys wailed and moaned above him in the jungle trees as if they were lamenting his fate. He was so hungry that he ate grass and chewed strips of bark. Sometimes he found some fruit that the monkeys had dropped and he ate this ravenously, reckoning that if they found it edible it would be safe for him too. When there was no fruit he dug up roots and chewed them, washing them down with rainwater which he found in plants like small cups.

But it was not enough and his strength was failing rapidly. He was in agony from his foot and could only crawl along. He had no fear that the Japanese would find him here, but his spirits sank lower and lower as each day passed and he had still not escaped from the jungle.

Then, all at once, he was clear of the stifling undergrowth and came out on to a track. He cheered up a little and followed the track all day. But his hopes were suddenly dashed when it ended at a huge tree stump. Nearby was an old collapsed hut in a small clearing containing an overgrown potato patch.

He sat down, miserable and exhausted, and wondered what he should do next. Eventually he decided to go back along the track and follow it to its source in the hope of finding some help there. Perhaps it would lead back to the road or to the house where he had seen the mongol boy in the cage. One thing was certain; he could not stay here, and by now he had not enough strength to get through any more jungle. The risks which the track would bring had to be taken if he was to stay alive.

Wearily he got to his feet and limped along the path. After a time he found that it was skirting a mountain which was so covered in jungle and thorny undergrowth as to be quite impassable. He gritted his teeth and forced himself on, knowing that this path was his last chance of survival. His mind was wandering now and his sight kept playing tricks on him so that he saw things where there was nothing and yet stumbled over obstacles that were plain to see. He felt as if a steel band was tightening round his chest and his breathing became more rapid. At dusk he could not go a step further and sank to the ground beside the path, panting and dizzy, and with a roaring in his ears.

He slept like the dead; which, indeed, at that moment, he very nearly was.

When he woke the next morning he was in a bad way and hardly knew what he was doing or where he was. With a great effort he struggled to his feet, choking down a cry of pain as his swollen foot took his weight. Like a drunken man he moved slowly on, reeling sometimes from one side of the path to the other.

Suddenly, round a bend ahead of him, six men appeared. He stopped, staring dully at them, his brain too numbed to drive his tired body into action. Too late to escape now, he thought bitterly, this is the end of it all. Motionless, he stood leaning on his stick, too exhausted even to draw his bayonet and put up a fight, and no longer really caring.

The men came closer and to his joy he saw that they were Chinese, carrying sacks of rice slung on poles. They clustered round and made signs of eating, beckoning him to follow them. With new hope, some strength flowed back into his body. Clenching his teeth he turned round and followed them back down the track. They soon reached a potato patch which he had already passed and here they turned off the track, walking up the potato rows to hide their footprints, and then pushing aside some cut branches which concealed a path through the jungle.

Hobbling along behind them, terrified that they would get out of sight, Jim pushed his endurance to its absolute limits. At last the path opened out into a jungle clearing where there were several well-built huts and about a hundred Chinese, some of them armed. Their Commander, who was in uniform and carried a .45 revolver in a holster, gave rapid orders and some men ran forward to help Jim while others went to fetch him food and drink.

When he had eaten, two men washed and shaved him and gently peeled the rotting sock off his wounded foot which they then dressed. They threw away his boots which had almost disintegrated and gave him a pair of white plimsolls. While they were thus ministering to Jim, the leader, who spoke some English, stood by and talked to him.

'Do you want to fight the *Japun?*' he asked.

'Yes,' replied Jim, 'as soon as my foot has healed, I shall be ready to fight, and I shall go on fighting the *Japun* until the English come back and drive them away.'

'Good!' said the leader and he went on to tell Jim that there were other British soldiers whom they had hidden in the jungle not far away, and he promised that as soon as Jim could walk he would be taken to join them.

Jim thanked him and explained that he owed his life to the Chinese who had so often helped him. The leader gave more orders and the men helped Jim to a good bed in one of the huts, giving him a pillow and a warm blanket.

As he lay there, feeling clean and full of good food, his foot dressed and comfortable for the first time for a month, he reflected on his continuing luck. A few hours earlier he had almost reached the point where there was nothing left but to fall exhausted beside the path and slowly die. And death would not have come peacefully; the ants and rats would have seen to that.

Now it looked as if he had a chance. With this encouraging thought, he drifted off to sleep.

CHAPTER FIVE

Back Among Friends

In the morning Jim hardly dared open his eyes in case the events of the last twelve hours had been a fantasy conjured up by his failing mind. Then the rough warmth of the blanket and the fact that he was dry convinced him that he had not been dreaming. He lay still because his body ached in every muscle and he lacked any strength to make a move. His companions had already risen and he heard them talking outside the hut as they went about their tasks.

Soon the two men who had washed him came in with some food, and while he ate it they again dressed his foot. They brought hot water and gave him another wash, and took away his filthy clothes. Telling him to rest, they left him wrapped up in his blanket.

During the day they brought him more food, and the leader paid him a brief visit. Apart from getting up to relieve himself occasionally, Jim lay and slept all day, and by evening he was feeling much better.

Nearly a week passed like this, while his strength grew daily and his foot became cleaner and much less painful.

One morning the leader told him that some British soldiers were coming to see him. A few hours later they arrived with Chinese guides. Two of them were Australians and the third, their leader, was Sergeant Tom Showell of the 2nd Loyals, who had been reported missing after the battle of Yong Peng. After some discussion it was decided that Jim would move to their camp in a fortnight's time, when his foot should have healed sufficiently for him to walk.

When they had gone Jim felt wonderfully cheerful. Grateful

as he was to the Chinese guerrillas who had taken him in, and glad of their company after his long weeks alone, nevertheless he was not really one of them and the prospect of being reunited with his own kind was very exciting.

The time passed quickly. Each day he walked a little in order to keep his muscles exercised and to prepare his foot for the journey. By the end of the two weeks he could walk quite easily; the wound was still open but was clean and healthy. Towards the end of March the guerrilla leader gave him some guides and the others smiled and wished him luck. Jim told them how grateful he was and for a moment he felt genuinely sorry to be leaving. The guides were anxious to be off so as to complete the journey in daylight, so, with a final farewell, Jim left the camp where he had been brought back from the brink of death.

All day they walked. In spite of his exercises Jim became very tired and his foot painful, but the thought of his destination spurred him on. At dusk they reached the camp. After the inmates had welcomed him, they gave him some rice balls and tinned meat. Then they gathered round him while he ate and listened to the story of his experiences. In spite of his exhaustion, Jim felt so exhilarated in spirit that he talked on into the night.

Like him, the other soldiers had been cut off in battles in north or west Johore. They had fought well and were very disappointed that the Japanese had managed to defeat them and to capture Singapore. They all hoped to be of some use behind the enemy lines until the British recaptured Malaya, which everyone thought would be only a matter of weeks.

There were about twenty of them all told, Privates Gooch, Guest and Crowe from the 6th Norfolks, Sergeant Tom Showell and Private Brian Smith from the 2nd Loyals and the remainder from the 2/29th Australian Battalion. Harry Crowe, Douglas Guest and Fred Gooch had been with Jim in the Rengit battle, although he had not met any of them until now. Gooch's hearing had been damaged by gunfire and, when orders came to withdraw from the Rengit water tower, he had not heard them and he had suddenly found himself alone among the Japanese. He had managed to slip away unseen and, following the road south, had passed through two road-blocks without being detected. Later he had joined up with some other lost soldiers.

Harry Crowe and Douglas Guest had run into an ambush two days after leaving Rengit during which Crowe had been shot through the calf of his left leg and their party of thirty men had been split up. He and Guest, who had known each other in India, made their way to Johore Bahru over the next two weeks, arriving the day after Singapore had fallen. Here they saw heavy concentrations of Japanese, so they returned to the jungle and headed north for about twelve miles. After a narrow escape from capture when they were betrayed by some Punjabi troops who were collaborating with the Japanese, they were picked up by two Communist Chinese guerrillas who eventually brought them to join Tom Showell, Brian Smith and some Australians in the jungle south of Layang Layang.

After Sergeant Showell had been cut off in the Yong Peng battle, he had gone south towards Singapore, gradually collecting a number of lost soldiers on the way. When news reached him that Singapore had fallen, he had taken to the jungle with his band of men, determined to continue his private war against the Japanese. Although he was the leader of the party, Jim saw that he was having a difficult time with some of the Australians, particularly with the Australian sergeant.

With the British and Australian soldiers were ten guerrillas who acted as guides and arranged supplies of food, as well as warning them of any Japanese patrols in the area. The soldiers had some rifles which they were determined to keep, although the guerrillas were always trying to get hold of them; Tom Showell gave Jim one.

Jim also noticed that everyone had dysentery and within a few days he himself was suffering from it. It was of a particularly virulent type and, even though he set off for the latrine at the first onset of stomach pains, he often fouled himself before he reached it. The stomach pains and soreness became progressively worse. Undoubtedly the fouling of the ground on the way to the latrine ensured that the men were continually reinfected. Strangely enough, considering the conditions under which he lived for the next three years, Jim never again suffered from this illness.

He handed over most of his money to the Chinese so that they could buy food for the party. Supplies were good at this time and he felt his body growing stronger each day as he rested and ate well.

During April the guerrillas said that the group must move somewhere else. The Japanese were consolidating their hold on the countryside and their patrols were getting closer and more frequent. Also, if they were to stay in any one spot for too long, there was a danger that they would be seen by Indians or Malays who would betray them to the enemy.

A day or two later the Chinese led the soldiers out of the camp and into the jungle. After a little while they passed through a swamp and came out into open country. Skirting around this, they got into a large rubber plantation before nightfall and arrived in the dark at a railway line. Just as they were preparing to cross it they heard a train in the distance so they hid behind the rubber trees.

The train clanked by, sending sparks flying up into the night. They could see armed Japanese guards sitting on the footplate and wagons. It seemed strange to Jim to see them passing so close and yet quite unaware of the eyes which watched them from the darkness under the trees. After the train had gone they crossed the line and found themselves once again in open country.

Jim began to feel rotten and he knew, from observing others in the last camp, that he was having an attack of malaria. Alternately sweating and shaking with cold, dizzy and with a splitting headache, he struggled on because he was well aware that it would have been suicide to stay in open country in daylight. Harry Crowe collapsed and his legs refused to work at all so the others had to take turns at carrying him.

They came to some tall elephant grass and took a path which ran through it. Suddenly a Chinese sentry stepped out of cover and spoke to the guides. The party went on and Jim noticed that a string of *rattan* ran along the edge of the path from the sentry to the camp. They heard a rattling of tins as the sentry pulled the *rattan* to warn the camp of their coming. Dawn was breaking as they entered a clearing containing a long row of huts and occupied by about twenty Chinese guerrillas.

The Chinese fed them on rice and gave them boiled water to drink. Exhausted by their day and night journey, they rested here for the next two days. They were then told that they must go to another camp in the jungle, but Crowe was allowed to stay until he was well enough to walk.

Chinese carriers were supplied to take the cooking pots and, soon after dawn, they set out once more. All day they travelled, seeing nobody and only a solitary *kongsi* house, through swamps and thick secondary jungle. In the evening they reached a well-used clearing which had in it many huts, a parade ground, meeting house and cookhouse, the latter by a stream. The soldiers sorted out space for themselves in the huts and settled down to domestic duties. Tom asked Jim to help in the cookhouse where the supplies consisted of sweet potatoes and dried fish paste (*bĕlachan*) out of which he made a foul-smelling, if nourishing, dish. As the stream was a little way from the camp, Tom suggested that Jim should hide his rifle there rather than in his hut because the guerrillas were very anxious to get hold of the rifles for themselves.

One day six Malays approached the camp early in the morning, saw the soldiers and ran away. Fred Gooch, who was collecting firewood for the cookhouse, dived out of some bushes at one of them but the Malay slipped through his fingers and ran off, leaving one shoe with Fred. This visit caused consternation among several members of the party who began packing their kit to leave, while Tom posted a sentry on the track along which the Malays had fled.

Before long the sentry heard a crackling of twigs in the distance. He rushed back to warn the others. Many of the soldiers started to panic and some ran out of the camp in the opposite direction. Tom managed to calm down the remainder and they took up good ambush positions and waited for an attack. The minutes ticked by and suspense mounted.

Suddenly, Japanese soldiers, led by the Malays, charged yelling out of the bushes and into the clearing. Tom and his men mowed them down, taking them completely by surprise. Before they could recover and launch another attack, the ambush party scrambled quickly away into the undergrowth.

They trotted down the track, confident that the Japanese would not follow them very closely. After passing through a small swamp, they caught up with the others just before dusk. Tom took them to task for running away, making it very clear that he considered they had put up a poor show.

They marched on in the dark in order to get well away before daylight, retracing their journey of a few days before. When they arrived back at the lone Chinese *kongsi* house the door was open and they entered cautiously. It seemed deserted but there was a wick burning in a jar of oil so they knew that the inhabitants could not be far away. They searched until they found some frightened Chinese civilians who gave them food. At first light they moved on again and eventually came to a tree felled across the path. A sentry appeared from the bushes and let them through to the camp, where they found everyone preparing to move because they had heard the shooting of the previous afternoon. Crowe had by now recovered the use of his legs and they all set off back through the elephant grass and into thick jungle.

Next morning the soldiers and guerrillas continued their journey, passing through swamps and wild rubber, and up and down hills. By dusk they had not reached their destination so they carried on in the darkness using small pieces of burning rubber as flares. These were not very effective and men were slipping and falling and cursing all the time as they slowly advanced.

Early in the morning they reached a large *kongsi* house. Here the guerrillas left them, saying that they would send in food the following day. Two of the guerrillas were detailed for this task, one of whom the soldiers nicknamed 'Tich'. He was a surly little rat of a man and, unusually for a guerrilla, was extremely unfriendly to the soldiers. Neither of the Chinese would live with them at the house, but they came in nearly every day with food of some sort.

Life in the *kongsi* house made Jim realize that once more his future was in jeopardy. In his days alone in the jungle, and when he had been with the Chinese guerrillas, he had yearned for company of his own race. But now that he had it, it was proving a mixed blessing; he was very worried by how much some of his companions grumbled and quarrelled. Nearly all of them were suffering from malaria, dysentery or beri-beri, and some had all three. The sick tended to lie about on the bed platforms all day, arguing with each other. The fit men took turns at sentry duty and, when they were free, bathed in the stream which ran very fast over several waterfalls. But the water was surprisingly cold and they could not stay in it long.

Although he was suffering intermittently from malaria, Jim decided that he would keep on his feet and try to occupy his time. They had now run out of food completely, so he wandered about in the jungle to see if he could find anything to eat. He enjoyed this; it gave him something to do and his childhood years spent with his gamekeeper father in the woods at Heydon were of great advantage to him. He found what appeared to be a pear tree with masses of fruit lying on the ground, but he noticed that it had not been eaten by any animal so he ignored it. He then saw a small turtle but was unable to catch it.

When he returned to the house an argument was raging among the men; some were saying that they would not stay there any longer, especially as there was no news of further food supplies. There were two factions in the camp. Tom Showell was prepared to co-operate with the Communist Chinese guerrillas but thought that the British and Australians should retain their weapons and act independently if necessary. A few of the Australians agreed with him but the rest, led by the Australian sergeant, were in favour of gaining the confidence of the Chinese so that they could be trusted with arms and ammunition. When this had been achieved, they proposed to set off and work their way north towards the Allied forces in Burma. The rift between the two sergeants thus split the Australians – on one occasion they even asked the Chinese to put them in separate camps, which the Chinese refused.*

To get away from the depressing atmosphere, Jim wandered off again, cutting marks on the trees so that he could find his way back. Eventually he came across the track along which the Chinese had brought them from the guerrilla camp, but he dared not stay on it so worked his way along a stream until he suddenly came to the jungle edge. For a little while he sat there enjoying the sun and a sight of the sky; it was like coming out of a dark cave into sunlight and fresh air, and he realized how unnatural and gloomy life was in the deep jungle.

As he sat there, listening and watching, he was suddenly aware of the sound of babies crying, and then, partly hidden by some trees on his left, he saw that there was a group of houses not far away. He thought it was too dangerous to go any nearer unarmed and alone, so he retraced his steps with the help of the

---

* The 2/29th Battalion had been engaged in the most savage fighting of the Malayan campaign in their six-day withdrawal from Muar during which they had lost thirteen officers and three hundred men. These survivors were physically and mentally exhausted. Sergeant Croft, an agressive man, bullied rather than led them and resented some of his men looking to Tom Showell for leadership. Other Australians did not like Tom Showell. Hence the low morale in the camps.

cuts he had made on the trees. He told Tom what he had seen and it was decided to send a party to the *kampong* to try and get some food.

The next morning Tom set off with Fred Gooch, Douglas Guest and Brian Smith. Jim led them to the jungle edge but, as the wound in his foot had opened up again during the fight with the Japanese, Tom told him to wait there in case they had to make a quick escape. The others crept through the bushes towards the houses and disappeared from sight. For an hour he sat still, listening and watching for the first sign of danger. Then the others rejoined him. Their news was not encouraging; the *kampong* contained some very poor Chinese who were terrified of the Japanese and who had little food. They had only been able to let Tom have some sweet potatoes and a few green vegetables.

The guerrillas had also produced a small quantity of potatoes but this was quite inadequate for the soldiers' needs. Tom told 'Tich' that they must have more food. The latter seemed quite uninterested and they felt sure that, had his leader not ordered him to get food for them, he would have done nothing about it and would have let them die.

The small ration was soon consumed and the men started complaining and arguing again. Jim never took sides; he was able to get on well with all of them, partly because he was worse off than they were, being the only seriously wounded member of the party, but also because he refused to quarrel.

Tom decided that they must go out again and look for other *kampongs* which might produce more food. He asked Jim to come again as he knew the country better than the others. They reached the jungle edge in daylight and waited until dark. As a landmark, they took note of a large dead tree stump where their path entered the jungle. From here a small path ran along the jungle edge and they felt safe in using this as the Japanese were unlikely to be out at night. The track ran up and down the slopes of low hills and in the valleys were streams which they crossed by putting logs across them. They passed a strip of cultivation on one hill and noted it with a view to picking up some vegetables on their return journey.

The first *kampong* they reached was a failure; the occupants bolted their doors and shouted at them. Seeing that they were Chinese the soldiers shouted back, '*Chiang Kai-shek, ini macham!*'

.(like this) and made a thumbs-up sign.* It was all they knew of the language at this time and they hoped it would ingratiate them with the villagers. But their words had no effect. They went on to another *kampong* but the result was the same; the Japanese had obviously terrorised them completely.

They walked along the jungle edge again and came to a third *kampong*. A small boy saw them coming and rushed away but shortly afterwards a Chinese girl appeared. She spoke some English and brought food, drink and cigarettes to them while they waited under cover a short distance from her house. She told them that she had been a hospital nurse in Singapore but that when the Japanese had burst into the hospital, bayoneting to death wounded soldiers in their beds, and then raping and killing Chinese nurses, she had hidden from them in a linen cupboard and made her escape that night. (This incident was the notorious Alexandra Hospital massacre of 14 February, 1942.)

The girl had walked to the north coast of Singapore Island, crossed the Johore Strait in a *sampan*, and eventually made her way to this *kampong*, called Tak Wah Heng, where her six brothers were living. She gave Tom and Jim some food and *hung yen* (red tobacco) to take back to the others and told them to come again if they needed anything. They warned her to watch out for Japanese patrols, who must on no account get to know that she was helping the British; she replied that if a patrol came anywhere near the *kampong* she would go and hide in the jungle. She seemed more concerned about the soldiers' safety, and it was agreed that she would burn a small lamp at night in the doorway to show that it was safe to come. If no light was showing, she insisted, they were to be very careful as the Japanese might have laid a trap for them.

It was time to go. Thanking her for her kindness, they retraced their steps and entered the jungle at the dead tree stump. They were so excited at having made this successful contact that they hardly noticed their weariness as they stumbled into camp at dawn.

The others were delighted with the food and tobacco, but both were soon finished. During the morning there was another

---

* At this time the British assumed that all Chinese, including guerrillas, were supporters of Chiang Kai-shek and not members of the Malayan Communist Party.

quarrel and three of the Australians said they were going to leave the party.

'We can't go on living like this,' they argued. 'We're prepared to try our luck outside.'

The others tried to persuade them to stay. 'What will happen to us,' somebody protested, 'if you get caught and give us away when you are tortured?'

However, the Australians were adamant and that evening they left, never to be seen again*

When the Chinese brought in food they were very disturbed by the departure of the three Australians but did not know what to do about it. Soon after this, Tom went out and found some more food but it was becoming scarce in the *kampongs* and he felt that the time was coming when the Chinese civilians would not be able to supply them any longer. Morale in the camp was very low and complaints to 'Tich' about the shortages had no effect at all. By now the sick were just lying listlessly on the communal bed platform day and night, grumbling about everything. The truth was that their life in the jungle was destroying their will to live. Tom decided to take out one more party. The two Norfolks, Fred Gooch and Douglas Guest, both of whom seemed fit, accompanied Tom and Jim that night to visit the Chinese girl at Tak Wah Heng.

They approached the *kampong* with great care, pausing frequently to look and listen. It was so silent that their suspicions were aroused. Then they saw that no light was burning in the girl's doorway. They crept silently to the first house; there was no movement or light inside so they withdrew into a dip in the ground where they lay quite still, their rifles ready to fire. The silence was oppressive. There was no movement anywhere except for the unsteady flickering of the fireflies. Something was not quite right; Jim felt his heart thumping and was sure that the others could hear it.

Suddenly the silence was shattered as a yelling party of Japanese erupted from one of the houses and charged towards them.

The soldiers opened fire rapidly and shot them down. More Japanese came running from behind other houses and they fired again, scattering them. Then the out-numbered British

* For details of the men in the camps, see Appendix.

jumped up and dashed into the jungle, pursued by a hail of
bullets none of which touched them. In their mad rush, they
were badly torn and scratched by thorns – the jungle is not a
place through which to move quickly in the dark.

They did not think that the enemy would follow them and,
after a little while, they stopped and listened. They could hear
the enraged Japanese shouting in the *kampong* and their wounded crying out with pain, but there was no noise in the undergrowth to suggest that they were being followed. However,
Tom Showell decided to take no chances. He told them to
reload and take cover in a hole left by an uprooted tree.

'You've done well,' he added quietly, 'keep calm now. If they
do come after us, empty your magazines at them and then
scatter. We shall probably become separated in the darkness so
make your own ways back to camp.'

They lay motionless for several minutes, straining their ears
to catch any sound of Japanese movements. Suddenly a
machine-gun opened up on them from the jungle edge. Bullets
ripped through the trees around the soldiers, but they lay still.
Then the firing stopped as suddenly as it had begun. For a few
minutes more they lay and listened, but there was no sound
from the Japanese so they crept out of their hiding place.

Tom whispered, 'I reckon the Japs will report back that
they've wiped us out. Let's get going.'

They walked quietly along the path, dodging back into the
undergrowth at regular intervals and listening. At last they felt
sure that they had shaken off pursuit and strode quickly along
the track. In their exhilaration at having worsted the enemy
their spirits rose and they felt more like the fighting soldiers
they had once been. Jim had been particularly impressed by
Douglas Guest's behaviour. He was a regular soldier who had
seen service in India and he had remained cool and efficient
throughout the most dangerous moments.

But their elation evaporated as they trudged homewards
wondering what had become of the Chinese in the *kampong*, in
particular the girl who had been so kind to them. Her fate was
not difficult to imagine.

They entered the jungle at their tree-stump landmark and
followed Jim's trail through the trees. They were suffering now
from fatigue caused by their poor diet, as well as from the
exertions of the battle. Their protectors, the Lee-Enfield rifles,

had become burdens, growing heavier and heavier and catching in the undergrowth at every step. But they had come to
regard the jungle as a friend rather than an enemy, and they
could reflect with pride on having escaped the Japanese trap by
their cunning.

It was beginning to get light when they staggered into camp.
They told the others what had happened, how they had nearly
been caught and had not brought back any food. The men
listened in silence to the story. Then they discussed what they
should do as the Japanese, furious at the failure of their ambush
and the loss of their men, would soon be searching the area in
large numbers. While they were talking, ten Chinese arrived
from the guerrilla camp. They said that three of their men had
been caught by the enemy who were operating around Tak
Wah Heng in strength. There had been pitched battles between
the Japanese and the guerrillas and many civilians had been
killed while others had fled into the jungle. The soldiers must
move at once, they insisted, and they collected up all the
cooking pots and started to leave.

It was a bad journey and particularly hard on the sick men
who had done nothing but lie about for weeks. They passed
through every type of country during the march: thick secondary jungle, swamps and open cultivation. All day it poured
with rain. At dusk they got into some jungle on a hill and lay up
for the night; then on again at dawn, up and down a succession
of jungle hills so steep that they had to pull themselves up the
slopes from one tree to another, slipping in the mud and dead
leaves underfoot and bruising their feet against tree stumps.

For Jim it was a dreadful journey; exhausted by his night of
battle, he now had trouble with his foot which was again
bleeding copiously and was covered with leeches. They came
down off the hills into a foul swamp where they floundered
through knee-deep slime for several hours. Jim was just beginning to think he would never reach the end of the day when all
at once they came out of the swamp and arrived at a guerrilla
camp. They threw themselves down on the ground completely
exhausted.

Chinese guerrillas kept arriving at the camp until there were
more than a hundred of them. They reported fighting with the
Japanese and were clearly worried by the numbers of the enemy
in the vicinity of Tak Wah Heng. However, they said, this camp

would be safe as it was too deep in the jungle for the Japanese to find it. It was certainly impressive: good huts, a cookhouse and the parade ground and meeting house which were an essential part of Communist camps even in the deepest jungle. The approach to the camp was along a stream and then out on to a tree trunk, so that no tracks were left. Jim was to notice in all their camps that clever concealment like this was automatic.

The soldiers were billeted in a low row of huts. Some of the Australians showed the guerrillas how to use Lee-Enfield rifles. By now the guerrillas had extracted most of the rifles from the party, as the sick men could no longer carry them, but they said they would be responsible for the safety of the soldiers. Jim couldn't help wondering whether the rifles were all that the guerrillas wanted, and if they would now just let the soldiers die.

The Chinese gave orders that the men were not to leave their quarters for fear of giving away the camp's position. They brought food to the huts every day. Jim found this confinement very irksome, but he was glad of a few days' rest to heal his foot. However, some of the other men began to go to pieces. Worn out by their illnesses and lack of food, their strenuous flight had been the last straw. They started quarrelling again and even fighting among themselves. Eventually, two Australians, one the sergeant, ran away from the camp and were not seen again.

The rest of them stayed there throughout May. Early in June the Chinese told them that the Japanese were moving large number of troops to Tak Wah Heng in order to attack the camp – they had probably found out about it by air reconnaissance – and that they would have to move on.

Harry Crowe was again unable to walk so they set off next morning carrying him on an improvised stretcher. Late in the day they came across a party of five Australians who were living in a hut so low that they had to crawl into it. There was no bed platform, the Australians just lying on the floor in their blankets. They said that the guerrillas wanted them to build themselves a proper hut but they could not be bothered as they might have to move on at any moment. The hut was very crowded and the atmosphere oppressive as they all came in to sleep. In the end they spent most of the night playing cards. Jim could see that the Australians were very unhappy and he did not think that they would survive for long. That night he had another attack of malaria.

The following day, accompanied by the five Australians, they continued their journey and by evening reached several small roughly-made shacks, widely spread in open country. They had originally been built and occupied by Chinese civilians who had fled there but who had now left ahead of the Japanese advance. The guerrillas gave the soldiers food and cooking pots and left them.

Tom, Douglas, Fred and Jim shared one of the huts in the new camp. It was in very bad repair and they had to patch the many leaks in the roof to keep out the almost incessant rain. But Jim enjoyed the company there. Douglas and Fred were not only men of the Norfolks but also about his own age, and Fred's dry humour helped them all to put up with the discomfort. Above all, Jim admired Sergeant Tom, and he learnt more about him over the weeks the four were together.

Tom Showell, the eldest of fourteen children, was a big man with dark brown curly hair and tattoos on his chest and arms. He had a strong personality and deep religious convictions, and was immensely proud of his regiment, The Loyals, whose honour he was determined to uphold. He had no patience with the growing defeatism and grumbling of some of the others, and he came more and more to depend on the Norfolk soldiers who, as he could see, also had good fighting qualities. Tom had served in Sarawak for a time and had a smattering of Malay and Chinese, so he naturally became the spokesman for the party in their dealings with the guerrillas. In spite of their depressing circumstances and the low morale of some of his men, he always remained cheerful and Jim remembers him going about singing 'Sarawaky skies are blue' and 'The little red caboose behind the train', which were his favourite tunes.

During July they moved yet again. They had little to do and Jim was unable to wander as much as he had done in the past, so he spent many hours at the ice-cold stream washing himself. He was determined to keep clean because he could see the demoralizing effect of dirt and disease. The Chinese continued to supply them with food – never enough – and time hung very heavy on their hands.

In the middle of August the guerrillas came and moved them again. Once more it was a long and gruelling march and the sick men made very slow progress. When they arrived at their destination they found that there were no huts, but the Chinese gave them sickles and *changkuls* and said that they would have to make their own. They gave them some food, then went away and left them to it.

The soldiers made the shelters on the same pattern as those in which they had lived in other camps, gathering and plaiting the *atap* fronds, pulling down *rattan* to use as ties, and building a platform three feet off the ground on which to sleep out of the wet and away from snakes and scorpions. But it rained heavily most of the time and they had to keep repairing their amateur thatching to stop the leaks. It was also cold at night and, as few of the men had blankets, they spent long hours awake and shivering. Most of them had malaria and dysentery by now, including the resourceful Tom. Their only food was *ubi kayu* (tapioca root) which the guerrillas brought for them, and they grew weaker and weaker on this diet.

Jim kept on his feet as much as possible. He helped some of the others build their huts when he had finished his own, and he was surprised how easily they took his help for granted. A few were now very ill with beri-beri and he carried water to them, collected firewood and cooked for them day after day. Some of the Australians with whom he got on well were grateful; the rest only grumbled.

By late October they were getting desperate for food. Jim went out again with some of the fitter men. They found a track which led to the jungle edge and thence to a vast pineapple plantation. Every day they collected pineapples and brought them back to the camp but eventually the fruit made their mouths quite raw and they had to give up eating them. All they had was the small quantity of potatoes which the guerrillas brought in, cooked in salt which had at last been provided in response to their frequent requests.

And then, one by one, the Australians began to die.

CHAPTER SIX

Death Shack

The end came so quickly for some of them that their companions were taken by surprise and could not understand why they had died so suddenly. Jim and those who were not very sick did everything they could for the dying, washing them and giving them food, but each death seemed to increase the despair of the other invalids who must have known in their hearts that there was now only one escape left to them.

It was a terrible time. The quarrelling and grumbling had ceased now; they no longer had the strength for it but just lay staring upwards until death overtook them. Two Australian brothers who had lain side by side all these weeks died within a few days of each other, first Frank Nippard, who was racked with malaria and grotesquely swollen with beri-beri, and then his brother George, whose heart was broken by his death.

Jim and the other men who could walk had to drag the bodies out of the shelters and bury them. The ground was so full of tree roots that they had to use the *changkuls* as axes in order to dig the graves. In their weakened state they were unable to dig further than was necessary just to cover the bodies. As each man died it seemed inevitable that they would all go this way in the end.

They were only about an hour's walk from the jungle edge and one day they heard a great deal of firing. Shortly afterwards a stream of Chinese women came running through their camp and on into the jungle. Tensely they waited, unable to move the sick men and hardly able to walk far themselves, but the Japanese did not follow the fugitives.

Late in November, Harry Crowe, whose leg wound had healed, and an Australian Private, 'Curly' Robertson, left the

camp to try their luck outside.* Both had escaped for a few
hours on a previous occasion but had been picked up by a
guerrilla and brought back. Tom Showell had been furious with
them and had threatened to kill them if they tried to escape
again. Robertson, 2/19th Battalion, had already escaped from
Changi with four other Australians late in March, 1942. After
crossing to the mainland in a small canoe they split into two
parties. Robertson and his companion, a man called 'Tich' of
2/20th Battalion, were soon betrayed by Malays. Robertson
managed to escape and was later picked up by Chinese guerrillas. He lived with them for two months before joining Jim's
camp.

Tom was now very ill, and the Chinese had not visited them
recently. Tom asked Jim and Fred Gooch to go and find the
guerrillas and tell them about the two soldiers who had left and
also about the Chinese women who now knew the camp's
location and might betray it to the Japanese under torture.
They were also to emphasize to the guerrillas the serious food
shortage and the many deaths which had occurred in the party.
Finally, if they met Crowe and Robertson they must persuade
them to return, because, with so many sick men, the camp
would be in great danger if these two were to be captured by the
Japanese.

In spite of their weakened condition, they agreed to go. Each
taking a rifle and two spare clips of ammunition, they set off in
daylight through the jungle until they came to the pineapple
plantation. They crawled through this, getting very scratched
in the process, and eventually reached the edge, where they
stopped to rest and to wait for darkness to fall.

The first houses which they checked were empty. Then they
visited another *kampong* and here they were stoned by the
inhabitants who seemed desperate that the Japanese should not
find British soldiers near them. Nowhere could they find any

* They wandered about for two weeks scrounging food and then were betrayed by
an Indian who cooked them a good meal and sent a message to the Japanese while they
ate it. After lengthy interrogation by the *kempeitai*, both were imprisoned in Changi.
Crowe persuaded the British authorities to send him out of Changi on a working party.
He was sent to the island of Blakang Mati, where he remained to the end of the war.
'Curly' Robertson also evaded the *kempeitai*. He arranged to be shipped to Japan,
narrowly avoiding death when his convoy was attacked by American submarines and
several ships were sunk. Meanwhile his unit in Singapore told the Japanese that he had
died. He survived the war and is alive today.

trace of the guerrillas and they were beginning to think that their search was of little use when they saw another *kampong*, not far from Poh Lee Sen. Crawling silently to within a few yards of the houses they lay in the bushes and surveyed the *kampong* in the moonlight. There was no sound or movement, nor any light in the houses, and, remembering the ambush which they had narrowly escaped on a previous occasion, they waited for some time, listening and watching. In the end they decided that the *kampong* was deserted. There seemed to be no signs of Japanese either, although the air was heavy with a sickly stench which puzzled them a little.

With Fred covering him, Jim inched forward intending to search the houses and look for food. The smell became nauseating as he got closer, and then he saw the cause of it. The Japanese had been there. Stuck on poles and hanging from trees were the heads of those they had executed, and even worse, tied to trees were the bodies of pregnant women who had been disembowelled so that their unborn children hung out between their legs. Many had also had their breasts cut off.

Retching with horror, Jim rushed back to Fred and, without explanation, told him to go back to the camp. After a few seconds, his mind still clouded by a sickened incredulity, Jim followed. The slaughter in the *kampong* confirmed all he had ever heard about Japanese atrocities.

Suddenly he heard the well-known chatter of an enemy patrol. Had they been betrayed by someone at the *kampong* where they had been stoned? Jim knew that Fred Gooch, who was ahead of him, had been deafened by a gunfire injury during the fighting in Johore and he saw, to his consternation, that Fred had not heard the Japanese. He picked up a lump of earth and threw it at Fred's back. The latter turned round and Jim signalled to him to take cover.

But his warning was too late; the Japanese, coming along the path, saw them both in the moonlight and opened fire on them. Neither was hit, and after a second's panic Jim followed Fred's example and coolly returned the fire. Some of the Japanese fell to the ground and the others scattered. Dodging among the houses and firing at intervals to deter the enemy from following, they reached some gardens and crawled through them. Then they saw ahead the gleam of moonlight on bayonets as two Japanese tried to cut them off. Shooting them down, they rose to their feet and dashed off into some *lalang* which gave them good cover. By the time they had got through this and back into the pineapple plantation, the shouting had died away and they knew that the Japanese had lost them.

They crawled through the pineapples, bleeding from many scratches, and came to an empty shack. Almost at once some Chinese civilians, terrified by the shooting, appeared. The soldiers gave them Communist salutes and tried to tell them what had happened. Two Chinese men ran away but the women nodded as if they understood before going off towards the jungle. Jim and Fred reached the jungle edge and waited for dawn before returning to camp.

They resolved not to tell the others of the battle for fear of spreading alarm, and Jim decided to say nothing to anyone about the ghastly atrocities which he had seen in the *kampong*. But they had to tell Tom of their fight as they had used up all their six clips of ammunition. Fred Gooch was elated by his brush with the Japanese and congratulated Jim on his part in it.

Later in the morning some guerrillas arrived and said they must move at once. There were no Chinese carriers and they had to carry all their own gear as well as to help the very sick men who were hardly able to move.

They started out through the jungle and before long arrived at the edge, which they followed for about three hours before turning into the jungle again where they soon came to several large huts. Originally many Chinese civilians had fled here but now these had all moved on. They stayed only for the night and then pushed on. During the march Jim had another bad attack of malaria and stumbled along in a dazed state, shaking with fever.

At dusk they reached a tumbledown hut. Here the thick jungle crowded in all around them and a dense canopy of foliage overhead shut out all sunlight and dripped water on them continuously. They were shut in a steaming tomb which stank of rotting vegetation and was infested with scorpions and huge centipedes which did nothing to improve the morale of the men who were all absolutely dead beat. This was the place they were to call 'Death Shack' and Jim had a premonition that few, if any, of them would survive there long.

'Tich' and another Chinese brought them some *ubi kayu* which was the only food obtainable at the time. For the sick men it was the final straw; the strenuous flight through the jungle from their previous camp had used up their last reserves of strength. Within a few days they started to die, two dying in one day alone. Jim, still weak with malaria and suffering frequent attacks, could hardly drag himself out to dig the graves. He was soon too weak to do even this and they had to resort to covering the dead with leaves and any earth which they could scratch up off the floor of the jungle.

In spite of his feebleness he was determined to keep on his feet for as long as he could and he forced himself to go for a daily walk. On one of these he came upon a good track about six feet wide. He collected some of the other men and they set off along it to see where it would lead them. But it went on and on without arriving at any habitation and in the end they had to turn back.

The sick men continued to die and soon even Jim found himself too weak with malaria to walk about any more. He lay on the bed platform next to an Australian called Jack who was in a coma, probably with cerebral malaria, and huge black ants, which they called 'death ants', crawled all over him. Jim had an even worse attack than usual and, feeling very dizzy, lapsed at last into unconsciousness. When, eventually, he woke up, the fever had left him. He got unsteadily to his feet and staggered outside the hut to relieve himself. When he returned he saw that the other men were staring at him in amazement, and he asked them why.

'You've been unconscious for four days, Jim, and we thought you had had it,' they replied. 'We had already dug your grave, a bit deeper than usual because we felt you deserved it.'

Jim grinned weakly at them. 'Thanks, but I'm not dead yet.'

Disturbed by his near approach to death, Jim prayed daily for survival and this consoled him. Feeling that he must get a grip on himself again, he took a half coconut shell and staggered off to the stream to wash. The water was so cold that it made him gasp but he felt refreshed in mind as well as body. When he got back to the hut he found that Jack had died; this was a blow as they had been good friends.

By the end of January, 1943, only eight out of those who had come to the Death Shack were still alive: Sergeant Tom and Brian Smith of 2nd Loyals, Douglas Guest, Fred Gooch and Jim of 6th Norfolks, Hector Stephens and Bill Pickering of the

2/29th Battalion and an Australian named Alan. Something
had to be done soon or they would all die there. They talked
together for a long time.

Tom, who had been their leader for so long and hitherto such
a tower of strength, said, 'Let's give ourselves up. I've had
enough of this. We stayed in the jungle so that we could help
when the British returned but now it's obvious that they aren't
coming, and anyway, we're far too weak to help them now, and
soon we shall all be dead.'

·The others stared at him, dumbfounded, wondering if he was
going mad. Tom, who had always been so strong and determined as their leader, was he going to pieces at last?

'After all we've been through,' they protested, 'we can't
surrender now!'

Jim then told them, for the first time, of the atrocities he had
seen in the last *kampong* he had visited. 'If that's what they do to
you when they catch you, they are not taking me alive!'

They were aghast at his account and even Tom agreed that
they must not surrender. They decided to talk to 'Tich' and the
other guerrilla and demand to see their leader.

After this conversation, and after talking to 'Tich' who
promised to pass on their request, the survivors felt a little more
cheerful. One day, wandering about in the jungle, Jim came
across another track and followed it with Fred and Douglas,
hoping to find food. The country here was fairly flat and they
had to pass through some swamps before coming to two
deserted huts at the jungle edge. Potatoes were growing in the
gardens. Digging, they found that no potatoes had yet formed
so they took the tops of the plants and brought them back to eat.
They found them quite appetizing and made several journeys
there over the next few weeks. Douglas and Fred, who still
seemed fairly strong, always went but Jim found that he could
only manage an occasional journey as it took all day to get there
and back.

While they were in this camp the guerrillas brought them a
letter from a Major Chapman* in which he said that he had

---

* This was the late Lt. Col. F. S. Chapman, DSO, author of *The Jungle is Neutral*,
who was operating at this time with the guerrillas in north Malaya. In his book he
makes reference to stories of 'strong bodies of British and Australian troops who were
still fighting the Japanese in Johore', but in fact these never existed except as small,
poorly armed parties of doomed men such as in this narrative. See also Appendix.

heard of them; he encouraged them to keep going and said that he would try to come south to see them. The guerrillas also brought a letter from a Major Barry* who was operating in Johore and who said that he hoped to meet them soon.

Although neither he, nor any of the others, had the faintest idea of who these men were, Tom sent a reply to each letter, via the guerrillas, and they all felt considerably cheered to think that there were others who were still fighting in the jungles of Malaya.

True to his word, 'Tich' brought the guerrilla leader to see them and they discussed the future. The soldiers asked him to take them into their camp as so many of them had died in the jungle and they saw no hope of surviving for long on their own in this horrible place. The leader told them that his forces were now much better organized than they had been in the past, and said he would try to arrange this. Meanwhile he ordered two Chinese carriers to remain with them, and they built themselves a hut about fifty yards away from 'death shack'. Jim often visited them and observed that they were able to survive on next to nothing and that they seemed happy to be in the jungle away from Japanese attacks.

Food was still a problem because of the Japanese domination of the *kampongs*, many of which were now deserted. One day Jim saw a wild boar, with huge tusks, but he had no rifle with him and this potential supply of meat escaped them. Then a mouse deer came nosing round the hut after potato peelings and Brian Smith shot it dead with Tom's .45 revolver. Hardly had the sound of the shot died away than their two Chinese carriers fled into the jungle and were seen no more. The deer made several delicious and nourishing meals for them and encouraged them to try and get more meat. They made traps of bamboo and *rattan* and caught rats which they cooked in the red ashes of a fire. But one rat, shared between eight men, did not go far towards satisfying their hunger or their need for protein, so they made spears out of table forks and collected lizards and frogs, both of which they found very good to eat. These modest and

* Major Barry. (See *Red Jungle* by John Cross). Cross says that food and money were sent to the soldiers. Jim saw the letter from Barry, to which Sergeant Tom replied, but saw no money or food. He assumes that the Chinese kept these for themselves, or used the money to buy supplies for the soldiers later.

Private E. J. Wright, 6th
Battalion, The Royal
Norfolk Regiment.
Photograph taken in 1941.

CQMS John Cross DCM,
Royal Corps of Signals.
Photograph taken in 1945.
(*Courtesy Mr Christopher Fish and
The Imperial War Museum.*)

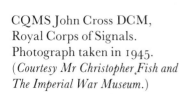

Private Fred Gooch, 6th Battalion, The Royal Norfolk Regiment. Died of fever, 19 July 1944 at Kambau, Johore. Photograph taken in 1941.

Sergeant F. Wagstaff, Royal Corps of Signals. Photograph taken after the war.

Private Harry Crowe, 6th Battalion, The Royal Norfolk Regiment. Photograph taken after the war.

Don 'Curly' Robertson, 2/19th Battalion, AIF. Photograph taken in Sydney, Australia, in November, 1945, after his release from PoW camp in Japan.

Lance-Sergeant Thomas Showell, 2nd Battalion, The Loyal Regiment. Died in 'Death Shack', 14 February, 1943. Photograph taken in Singapore in 1941.

Major Hart's camp, May 1945. Jim Wright is standing in the left
foreground. Behind him are Sergeant Roberts, USAAF, and Major
Hart.

Jim Wright and his wife went aboard *HMS Thule* when she visited
Lowestoft in May, 1958. (*Courtesy Norfolk News Co Ltd.*)

unusual additions to the menu helped, and there were no more deaths for the time being.

One day they were horrified to hear voices and quickly hid in the jungle. They saw three Chinese who were working down the stream catching fish by putting a poison, (derris root), into the water. This paralysed the fish and made them easy to catch by hand. The soldiers seized the Chinese as they dared not let them go away and possibly betray their whereabouts to the enemy. Although the men seemed quite friendly, they took no chances and guarded them day and night. The fish they had caught made a welcome meal for everyone. After a few days the two Chinese carriers, looking rather sheepish, returned. They questioned the three fishermen, and then released them, assuring the soldiers that they were trustworthy.

Then suddenly, in spite of their improved diet, disaster struck them again. First, Tom died. Since November, 1942, he had been afflicted by severe attacks of malaria and these gradually reduced his strength until he was unable to stand any longer. The men of the Norfolks nursed him devotedly, going out to get potato tops for him, and feeding and washing him. But he continued to go downhill and by early February he had become quite delirious. Eventually he slipped into unconsciousness and died a few days later.

Tom's death shook them badly. He had been a source of strength and leadership through all this grim period; now this had been withdrawn from them. Jim in particular mourned the loss of a friend. Numb with grief, they buried him alongside the others who had died in this ominous place.

Death had not yet finished with them. Soon after Tom's death the two Australians, Alan and Bill Pickering, died within a few days of each other from such bad attacks of malaria that they seemed to have gone raving mad. The survivors were now down to five.

Of those remaining, Douglas Guest and Fred Gooch still seemed reasonably well, and Jim was getting stronger than he had been a few weeks earlier. Brian Smith, who was only seventeen or eighteen, had held up splendidly throughout the three and a half months in the death shack, but, like the rest, he was subject to severe bouts of malaria. Hector Stephens was now the most seriously ill; a schoolmaster in Australia, bald and older than his companions, he had displayed great fortitude through a succession of illnesses. Never once did Jim hear him quarrel or complain and he greatly admired his cheerful acceptance of so much suffering. Now Hector was unable to walk as he was stricken by wet beri-beri as a result of vitamin deficiency. His body and limbs were grotesquely swollen and full of fluid and his scrotum was a bloated weeping mass the size of a football.

In April, 1943, the guerrillas came to the camp and said that they were going to move them to their headquarters, and that they would send men to carry Hector Stephens on a stretcher. The three Norfolks and Brian Smith set off with the Chinese. They went to the jungle edge on the same track which they had explored some weeks previously. It was a hard march and it rained all day which made the paths very slippery. But they were filled with hope and glad to have left that horrible camp behind them forever.

Jim's wound was still open and leeches kept getting into it but the Chinese had shown them how to burn leeches off with a glowing stick or a cigarette end and had warned them never to try and pull them off. All the soldiers suffered from deep septic ulcers in their legs, some of them down to the bone; these had all been caused either by leech bites or by scratches which had turned septic. Their diet, which was deficient in both proteins and vitamins, had lowered their resistance so much that every wound became infected. (These ulcers were a very common feature among POWs working in the jungles of Siam. Hundreds of leg amputations were necessary to save lives).

Jim, weakened by malaria, found it hard to keep up with the others. He was a living skeleton, weighing only about six stone – his comrades called him the invisible man – and he had no reserves of strength left with which to tackle such an arduous journey. He kept falling behind the others and was sometimes reduced to crawling when he became too dizzy and exhausted to stay on his feet. And all day the rain poured down soaking them to the skin.

By the afternoon they had come out into more open country where there was a mixture of jungle, *kampongs* and cultivation. The guerrillas seemed to feel safe here and kept to the paths, which made progress quicker and easier. They crossed one or two roads and went over the Sungei Sayong where they saw some Chinese making latex rubber into strips. These did not seem at all surprised at being visited by British soldiers, and they gave them some shoes made out of rubber. The shoes were very sloppy to walk in but they had the advantage of being washable, so they did not cause foot-rot as conventional boots and socks were liable to do.

They came to a deep ravine and had to cross by walking on a tree which had fallen across it. Jim was too dizzy for this and had to crawl across on his hands and knees. Soon afterwards they entered thick jungle and here the Chinese left them, telling them to make themselves a shelter. Luckily, in this jungle, there were wild banana leaves which measured about six foot by three foot, and they quickly made a roof of these and put more on the ground for bedding.

The next day the Chinese carried in Hector on a stretcher. Jim wondered how they had found the strength to walk and carry such a load over such difficult country. Before the Chinese left, the soldiers asked them when they would be able to join the guerrillas in their camp and were told that one of the leaders would come and see them soon.

The Chinese brought them *ubi kayu* occasionally, but the stream was down a steep hill and some distance from their shelter. They had to take turns at carrying water up, and they also had to get enough to wash and cook for Hector Stephens who was unable to move. Jim found that the journey here had used up all his strength and on his trips between the hut and the stream he had to rest frequently; his legs felt as if they were made of jelly.

After a few days a guerrilla leader from the 4th Guerrilla Regiment came to see them, bringing a large packet of *hung yen* tobacco. They talked for a short time and he agreed to have them moved soon to the 4th Regiment camp. This news, and the tobacco, cheered them immensely but they were worried about Hector Stephens whose beri-beri was getting worse. He was wonderfully brave and never complained although life must have been misery for him. He urged them to take the opportunity of going if it arose, but the others repeatedly assured him that they would not leave him behind. The weeks dragged on and there was no further sign of their move to the guerrilla camp. They became depressed again. Hector needed good food and medical attention urgently if he was to survive. Jim and Brian could do little more than take their turns as water carriers, as they could not shake off the malaria which now seemed to be with them always. Fred and Douglas went out twice and found some vegetables and pineapples by a hut in the jungle, but nothing more nourishing.

Towards the end of May, they heard voices early one morning and discovered five Chinese who had at last come to escort them to the camp.

'What about Hector?' Douglas asked. He had assumed the leadership after Tom's death as he was the most experienced soldier among them.

'One man go with four *Ingping* (English soldiers) and four men carry Hector and pots and pans,' one of the Chinese replied. He explained that Hector's party must go off first as they had to take a longer and safer route with him.

Later the other four set off with their guide and, soon after leaving the jungle, were moving across open country, partly rubber plantations and partly swamp. Douglas and Fred were still strong and Brian had recovered a little. Jim knew that he was the weak link but he was determined to make one more big effort now that safety seemed almost within their grasp. None of them was armed now as the Chinese had taken their rifles and even the .45 revolver with which Brian had shot the deer. Jim accepted that the surrender of their weapons was the price they had to pay for going to live with the guerrillas and, much as he regretted the loss of his rifle, he knew that they would not have lived for much longer on their own in the jungle. Once they had all died, the Chinese would have got their weapons anyway.

They spent that night near Kampong Rantau Panjang and the next morning joined some more Chinese who carried their gear for them. They had to cross the Sungei Johore which was bridged by a huge tree trunk, below which there was a considerable drop into the torrent. Jim felt very unsteady on this and, halfway over, began to sway on his feet. But his luck was still holding as a guerrilla behind him managed to grab and support him until they reached the other side.

They did not stop for the night but kept going in the dark on a good path until they reached the Sungei Lebah, which they crossed in a small boat. Soon afterwards they came to a narrow-gauge mining railway near Kuala Sisek and loaded themselves on to a flat-bottomed four-wheeled trolley. They went very quickly downhill but had to stop frequently because of landslides which blocked the track. The Chinese carried the trolley round each block and pushed the soldiers up the gradients.

Jim, who had another bad bout of malaria, sat shaking on the trolley as it careered along, but at least it was better than walking. At Tengkil they stopped at a hut belonging to Cheong Khuen, who worked as an engine fitter at the tin mine. He was a genial character, and a useful one, and they were to see more of him later. The line ended at the Sungei Tengkil; on the far bank, across a fragile bridge, was Kampong Tengkil. Here they stopped for the night.

Tengkil is a tin-mining area, and at the mining camp, which they reached next day, one of the houses had been turned into a hospital. Here Jim and Brian stayed in order to recuperate, while Fred and Douglas, who were in better shape, pressed on to the 4th Guerrilla HQ. By a tragic irony, Hector, who was most in need of medical treatment and was so nearly within reach of it, never made it but died while he was being carried to Tengkil on a stretcher, and was buried by the wayside.

The food at the hospital was good; there was quinine, stolen from the Japanese, for their malaria, and the doctor treated their ulcers with a kind of poultice made from leaves which drew out the poison. The legs of the Chinese in the camp were in no better condition than the soldiers; and as an alternative to the leaf poultices, applied a black paste called *Kow Yok* which was held together with rice paper. But perhaps the greatest luxury of all was the red woollen blanket which Jim was given: it was a lot better than the old rice sack, and he used to roll himself up in it at night and was warm at last.

After the gloom of the jungle, the sandy clearing was quite dazzling, and it took them a little time to get used to it. But as they recovered their strength, Jim and Brian felt the need for exercise; they went for walks and helped out at the local sawmill. Sometimes they went down to the *kampong* to exchange smiles and nods with the villagers, or watched the mineworkers sifting the sand for tin. On one of their expeditions Jim walked into a quicksand and only just managed to throw himself back before he was engulfed. Round the *kampong* the villagers grew groundnuts which they allowed the men to dig – a surprise to Jim, who thought they grew on trees.

Dominating the site was the house which had formerly

belonged to the English manager; now it served as a canteen where they could get a decent meal. Bit by bit they started to pick up the languages. The contrast with their hideous, fugitive life of the past sixteen months was a tonic in itself, and no one in the camp seemed to fear Japanese intrusion.

But the enemy were not far away, and Fred and Douglas reported, when they came to see Jim and Brian, that the guerrilla HQ was a ferment of activity, with armed parties sallying out to harry the Japanese, or returning from one sortie or other.

During their time here Jim learned something of Brian's unusual background. He told Jim that he had spent his childhood in China and, when the Japanese army had drawn near, his parents had sent him away. He had fled via Hongkong to Singapore where he had enlisted in 2nd Loyals, falsifying his age because he was only about seventeen.

His Company was at the Yong Peng defile position when the Japanese attacked and overran them on the afternoon of 23 January, just as they were preparing to withdraw. Some survivors struggled back through swamps and jungle to rejoin 2 Loyals at Yong Peng but Brian and Tom Showell arrived to find the Japanese in possession of the town so had to trek further south.

Brian was very worried about the fate of his parents, of whom he had heard nothing since leaving China, and he was determined, if he survived the war, to return to China to look for them.

After three weeks at Tengkil the doctor gave the two men a reasonably clean bill of health, and said they were fit to travel. It was now the third week in June, 1943; and, greatly restored in both mind and body, they left Tengkil with their guides to join the others at 4th Guerrilla HQ. A new and intriguing chapter in their adventures was about to begin.

CHAPTER SEVEN

The Guerrilla Camp

They set off along paths through the padi fields. These paths could be flooded at will so that no trace of their tracks would remain. Once again Jim noticed how clever the Chinese were at concealing their movements.

Entering the jungle they soon came upon a hut which was being used as a hospital by the guerrillas. Without stopping they plunged into a swamp, where they had to walk on rafts of floating bamboo, and as they clambered out at last on to dry land they were met by a sentry. He operated the usual alarm system of *rattan* and empty tins and directed them to a small bridge over a stream. Although they had been walking for about four hours, Jim was pleased to find that he still felt quite fresh. Crossing the bridge, they entered the guerrilla camp.

This was situated in a valley and alongside it ran a stream which supplied the camp with water. There were several houses, the usual parade ground and meeting house and, near the stream, a cookhouse and dining hut. The guerrilla leaders lived at the top end of the camp but Jim and Brian were taken to a hut near the cookhouse where they found Fred Gooch and Douglas Guest. The camp was well-organised and food was plentiful. There were two meals a day, mostly of vegetables with fish paste or dried whitebait, and the British soldiers ate with the guerrillas, sitting on the ground and helping themselves out of a communal pot. Once they had a turtle, which was delicious. Although they tried to use chopsticks they found that they could not eat with the same speed as the Chinese so reverted to the use of their spoons. In time their muscles grew strong enough for them to squat round the food in Chinese fashion.

Their relations with the Chinese were excellent. There were over a hundred guerrillas living in the camp; as their names were quite incomprehensible to the soldiers they gradually gave nicknames to those whom they came to know well. One non-Communist Chinese civilian was brought into the camp in handcuffs by the guerrillas. He had apparently committed no crime, but perhaps he knew too much and they could not risk his being interrogated by the Japanese. The soldiers immediately named him Janker Wallah and he became a firm favourite of theirs. Douglas remembered the term from his service in India; it was what the British Army called a soldier sentenced to extra drills and fatigues.

The four men helped in the cookhouse and prepared food; taking axes, they roamed about in the jungle cutting down dead trees, rolling the trunks down the hillside and then splitting the wood for the cookhouse fires. With so many men in the camp this was a full-time occupation as the cooks used a great deal of wood. But in spite of their improved diet they were all, Jim in particular, very emaciated and before carrying loads of wood they had to pad their shoulders to protect their protruding bones. By now their feet were quite hard and they only wore their rubber shoes when they were in thick jungle.

But they were always wet; soaked either by sweat or by rain, and although they got used to it they never liked it much. The camp stream was a boon. When they were not working they spent most of their time bathing. They deepened and enlarged a pool which they then surrounded with *atap* for privacy.

The Chinese, a very clean race, also washed themselves frequently in the stream. They used small towels with 'Good Morning' printed in red on them, in English at one end and in Chinese at the other. When they cleaned their teeth they scraped the top surface of their tongues with pliable strips of metal which they kept attached to their toothbrushes. Altogether, hygiene in the camp was of a high standard. The latrine was well away from the huts and well clear of the stream. It consisted of a six-foot-deep pit, stinking and writhing with maggots, over which they crouched precariously on logs thrown across it. Having no paper the English used selected leaves, but the Chinese preferred pieces of stick.

The two Chinese cooks, with whom the soldiers spent a lot of time each day peeling mountains of potatoes, taught them some Malay and also tried to introduce them to the various Chinese dialects. They picked up a lot of Malay, but the Chinese language baffled them. In return they taught the Chinese some English and, as a result, they were soon all able to understand one another. These cooks, Hailam Chinese* civilians, were not Communists but were just hiding from the Japanese, so there was no political tension between them and the British, which made for a friendly atmosphere.

Laborious though these conversations were, there was a sound reason for persevering with them. Although Jim some-times talked to Fred Gooch about Norfolk and the latter's work on a farm, and Douglas Guest spoke occasionally of his peace-time service in India in the Royal Norfolk Regiment, by tacit consent they kept off the subject of life at home as much as possible. Such talk led to homesickness which in turn gave way to depression, and this could be as much a killer as illness. They had seen too many men give up hope and die from despair, thinking only of their homes and families. (This same disabling nostalgia operated with POWs too, especially the younger ones.)

The protein content of their food was becoming a problem. Because of the absence of jungle fruit trees there were no monkeys near the camp. At various times they ate dogs, cats, snakes, bear and squirrel, and they continued the spearing of frogs, which they had learned in the Death Shack. Much of their protein was in the form of *bĕlachan* which they found nauseating in both taste and smell, although it may have been good for them. After a time they discovered that fresh-water shrimps lived in the stream, and they managed to catch them in the flat baskets which the Chinese used to sift tin.

Wild bananas grew in the area, and as the numbers of men in the camp increased continually, there was a great demand for their enormous leaves to roof new huts which had to be constructed. The soldiers helped in this, holding the leaves in place with bindings of *rattan* creeper which they pulled down from the jungle trees and split into ties. This splitting is quite an art, as the creeper has no grain, and the knife has to be kept absolutely straight; but the result, when the skill has been

* Chinese from the Island of Hainan.

mastered, is as strong and flexible as cord. The banana leaves also made very useful umbrellas on the rare occasions when the men were dry and wished to remain so.

Working with the Chinese like this not merely got the soldiers fit again and helped to pass the time, but established a cordial relationship with their hosts. It also helped to dispel the natural fear and depression which the jungle had induced in them in their earlier days. They were now quite attuned to jungle life and felt that they could survive it for a long time.

But as their bodies strengthened, they began to grow restless and longed to escape from the camp and indeed from the jungle itself. For their liberty was only nominal; effectively they were in the captivity both of their hosts and of the country, and it filled them with an oppressive claustrophobia. The jungle was a prison in itself.

At this time the guerrillas were rather short of carriers to bring in food supplies for the camp, so the soldiers asked if they could join the carrying parties. To begin with the guerrillas emphatically refused, afraid no doubt that the soldiers might be captured by the Japanese. But finally they agreed, and the four men set off at dawn the following day.

They carried individual loads slung over their shoulders so that some of the weight was in front of them and some behind, leaving their hands free. The Chinese, who always carried loads slung on a pole with an equal weight on each end, laughed at the soldiers' method and allowed them to carry only what they could easily manage. Jim found that he was still not as strong as the others and his loads were the smallest of all.

They went down to Tengkil sands and on to the bridge over the Sungei Tengkil which they had crossed during their journey from the Death Shack in May, 1943. Here there was a hut full of stored potatoes from which they made up their loads. They made several journeys with the carriers over the next few weeks, sometimes calling on the Chinese at Tengkil sands who had been their friends when they stayed there. Journeys lasted all day and, after a bathe and a meal, they had no difficulty in sleeping soundly.

One day, while collecting wood in the jungle, they came upon a small hut which was well-concealed in a dense thicket of *bertam*. In the hut they found, to their astonishment, six four-gallon cans of white sugar. This store had obviously been hidden by the guerrillas so that, in the event of a sudden Japanese attack on the camp, some supplies would not fall into their hands. It was a great temptation; they knew that if they were caught stealing the sugar the penalty would be death but, after so long on a low-calorie diet, they had a permanent and exaggerated craving for sweet things. They took their spoons with them several times and removed a small amount out of each can, while keeping a close watch outside. They realized that the guerrillas would soon suspect them if the level of sugar were to fall by any noticeable amount, so before long they had to stop visiting the hut. But they felt a great deal better for it.

One of their duties in the camp was to teach the guerrillas to use the rifles which they had taken from them. They found that the Chinese were quite hopeless as marksmen as they did not seem to be capable of closing one eye at a time; either both were closed or they squinted down the rifles with both eyes open. In the end the soldiers realised that they would never be able to train more than a few Chinese to shoot accurately and they reluctantly concluded that the only chance the guerrillas had of inflicting casualties on the Japanese would be in ambushes, firing at point-blank range and then bolting off into the jungle before the Japanese could retaliate. Although they laughed with exasperation among themselves, they knew it was no laughing matter as they were completely dependent on the guerrillas for their safety.

The Chinese were little better at marching, their limbs being quite un-coordinated as they walked up and down the parade ground shouting, 'it-it-it-erh-it' (1-1-1-2-1). Douglas Guest, a regular soldier, wondered what his old Sergeant-Major in India would have done if he had had to drill these Chinese.

As part of their political indoctrination the guerrillas spent the evenings, when not studying Mandarin, in putting on plays or singsongs. Both these were politically orientated, the Japanese always being portrayed as the 'baddies' and inevitably biting the dust while the victorious Chinese received not a scratch. The soldiers, for want of anything better to do, took part in the singsongs and learned the songs by heart. Jim used to do a solo rendering of a Malay song entitled '*Adek-Abang*' ('Sisters and Brothers'). The Chinese would retaliate with '*Prow-Young-de-Hunchie*' ('Beautiful Red Flag'), or '*Tongsaman-*

Tongsaman-Kwai-Che-Lie' ('Comrades, Comrades, Wake Up Quickly').

No doubt the more doctrinaire Communists regarded the soldiers' participation as a triumph for their political propaganda; they did not, in fact, understand the British soldier at all. As far as the Communists were concerned, he came from the working classes and was therefore oppressed, and so was suitable material for conversion to their ideas of world revolution. These particular soldiers must have been a sad disappointment to them; they took part in everything in the most commendable way, learning and singing the revolutionary songs, showing courtesy and friendship to their Communist hosts – and not the slightest interest in their political theories.*
Indeed, with the penetrating observation of the rank and file on matters of privilege, they saw that the Communist ideal of all men being equal was constantly abused. For example, Jim noticed that it was quite common for the Committee to have coffee and cigarettes when there was nothing but water for the rest of them.†

During this period the soldiers' health remained fairly good, but the improvement was precarious, and to some extent illusory. Their diet was not good enough to build up their stamina. But at least there were fewer mosquitoes here; and for as long as the Japanese did not bother them, they were able to keep a smoky fire going all night to sleep round.

A guerrilla raiding party had managed to capture an ox from the Japanese. This was eventually brought by jungle paths to the camp. Jim and the others went out with planks to put over the streams, where there were normally only tree-trunk bridges, so that the ox could be safely brought across them. Although it made a change to their diet it was so tough that they had great difficulty in eating it. The best part was the blood which they drained off and allowed to set in a jelly, but they also

---

* 'What the Chinese really thought of me I do not know; but certainly I was a source of considerable interest. . . . I believe it was a great source of surprise and disappointment to the guerrillas that, though I identified myself with them as comrades in arms, I made no attempt to accept their party views or aspirations and absolutely refused to discuss politics.'

The Jungle is Neutral by Lt. Col. F. Spencer Chapman DSO, 1949

† The fact was that the Chinese, unlike the Japanese, had always been noted for their sense of humour and good nature. The humourless Communist doctrine was ethnically quite alien to their characters.

chewed bits of the hide which, although tough, allayed their permanent hunger.

In spite of their settled life, the possibility of a surprise Japanese attack was accepted by both guerrillas and British. In order to avoid the loss of their few but vital possessions in such an event, they had developed a set routine. Every morning they rose at dawn and at once rolled their belongings into a ground sheet. This bundle was then placed in a square of cloth, secured by knotting two corners, and the remaining corners tied to make a loop which would go over a shoulder. Thus each man was ready to snatch up his bundle and dive into the jungle in the event of an attack. The only items kept out were a half coconut shell and a towel no larger than a handkerchief so that they could wash or eat during the day without undoing their bundles. The towels also served as pillows during the night.

One day the soldiers were delighted to meet Cheong Khuen, the diesel fitter from Kampong Tengkil. He had come to the camp to fix up a diesel engine which had been brought from the Tengkil tin mine so that the camp could have electric light. There was little risk in using this as the Japanese did not fly at night, nor did their troops go far into the jungle during the hours of darkness.

Later in the year Cheong Khuen was to join them permanently. While living in Tengkil he had been in the habit of making regular trips to Kota Tinggi to shop for the Tengkil community. Eventually he was picked up by the Japanese. During interrogation they learned that he was a civilian engine fitter from Tengkil. They became very interested and asked him if he would return there and persuade the miners to supply tin to the Japanese. Seizing on this chance of escaping from prison, he agreed, but added that he must have rice and other stores to take back to Tengkil so that he could bribe the miners. These the Japanese supplied and he went home in triumph with his booty.

However, as the Japanese now knew him by sight, he decided that it would be unsafe for him to go on living in the village, so he moved in with the guerrillas. In spite of their mutual antipathy, the arrangement suited both parties. He was very useful to them as a technician, but he was not allowed to take any part in their meetings. As he had worked for the British before Malaya was overrun by the Japanese, he got on very well with the soldiers and probably regarded them as an insurance for his future in the rather strained ideological relations which existed between the Communist leadership and himself.

The four men helped him to install the wiring for the lights and Jim, with his knowledge of lorry engines, was able to give Cheong Khuen some assistance in setting up the engine in a hut just uphill from their own. Here also lived Ah Gui, the black-smith/armourer. This man was fascinated by explosives, but his enthusiasm outran his knowledge. On one occasion he had nearly bled to death when he had blown the tips off all the fingers on one hand while experimenting with grenades. Un-daunted by this setback, he continued to fiddle about with explosive devices and the soldiers, who often visited him, would suddenly remember more urgent business elsewhere whenever they saw him reaching out for some lethal project on which he was working.

One of the two runners who took messages between guerrilla camps and detachments was called Ah Sing and was a great friend of the soldiers. He always managed to bring them a little tobacco when he returned from inhabited areas, and this was extremely welcome as it was always scarce in the camp. They constructed what they called a 'Hubbly Bubbly' (water-cooled pipe) out of bamboo, and they used to sit round taking single sucks at it before passing it on. The tobacco was so strong that it made them dizzy and their eyes streamed with tears.

Before long Ah Sing was sent to some armed non-Communist Chinese – always called *orang samun* (robber men) by the Communists – with a message suggesting that they should join up with the 4th Guerrilla HQ. This band shot at the two runners and killed Ah Sing. When the news got back to the camp a huge Chinese Communist, who carried a Bren gun as if it were a toy and whom the soldiers had christened 'OC Troops', borrowed a Tommy gun with which to exact revenge. Because of their friendship with Ah Sing, the soldiers asked 'OC Troops' if they might go with him, but he replied that it was too far. The next day he returned with the leader and deputy leader of the band, whom he had trussed by running a rope from their necks to their wrists which were bound behind them. Later they were executed.

As the number of men in the camp increased, the British had to share their hut with two Chinese. One of them kept to himself and spent all his time writing, but the other worked as a tailor and was very good to the soldiers, making Jim a cotton shirt and shorts to take the place of his Army uniform. As he had been wearing this continuously for eighteen months, it was now little more than tattered rags. In the next hut lived 'Tich', their hostile carrier from the 'Death Shack' days. He had not improved and always treated them in a condescending manner, but they had so many other good friends among the Chinese that they could afford to ignore him.

One day the guerrillas brought a Gurkha soldier to them. He spoke fair English and they were able to have a long conversation. They were amazed at how fit he was. He had many advantages over them, as far as survival was concerned, because he was able to pass as a native and to get supplies from the Chinese without arousing the suspicions of the Japanese or their collaborators. He asked them, if they ever managed to make contact with anyone in authority, to report that he was 'soldiering on' and waiting for the day when the British would drive the Japanese out of Malaya. He left them that evening and they never saw him again.

Then two Chinese girls arrived in the camp. Their job was to teach the guerrillas to read and write so that they could more readily absorb and disseminate Communist propaganda.

But, with the constant coming and going of guerrillas and other visitors, it was inevitable that the Japanese would eventually trace their HQ. The Chinese dug deep traps in the paths leading to the camp and the soldiers sharpened long staves of teak which they fixed in the bottom of the pits. These traps were then covered over with branches and leaves until they were invisible. For a time these pits, adapted by the guerrillas from those made by the Sakai – one of the shy, aboriginal, jungle tribes – to catch wild pigs, were very successful and many members of Japanese patrols fell into them and severely injured themselves. But after a time they developed the habit of sending natives ahead of them so that it was these unfortunates who received the injuries instead of the Japanese.

Late in November the Chinese told them that other British soldiers were coming to see them. This was exciting news as they had met no one of their own race since leaving the 'Death Shack' camp. After a few days Major Barry* (who had written

* 'Major James Barry' was a 'cover name' for Captain L. P. T. Cauvin, Intelligence Corps.

to Sergeant Tom the previous year), accompanied by CQMS John Cross and Sergeants Wagstaff and Morter, arrived in the camp. For some time, in fact, they had been living not far away, but the Chinese, for reasons of their own, had not allowed any contact between the two groups.

The visitors seemed amazingly fit and well-fed, and as they ran a secret radio station they were able to give the four soldiers a great deal of information. Jim and his companions were absolutely dumbfounded to learn that not only had the Japanese overrun Malaya and Singapore but they were now occupying the whole of South-East Asia from Burma almost to Australia. This was their first real news for two years, and the only encouraging item in it was that the Americans, having checked the Japanese advance of 1941/2 by their naval victories at Midway and the Coral Sea, were now gradually pushing the enemy back towards the Philippines. In Burma the Allies seemed to have made no progress in driving out the Japanese, although General Wingate had successfully carried out a daring operation behind the enemy lines. In Europe, the Axis had been defeated in North Africa and Sicily and the Italians had surrendered, but the Germans still occupied Italy and heavy fighting was taking place there. The Russians, having checked the Germans outside Moscow during the winter of 1941–2, were now beginning to regain lost ground and had had a notable success at Stalingrad where they had surrounded and destroyed a whole German army.

After listening eagerly to all this, the soldiers realized that they might have to survive in the jungle for several years before Allied forces could rescue them. Disappointing though this was, it was good to know that the tide of war was turning at last and to feel in touch, however faintly, with a world which they had almost forgotten existed.

Before leaving, John Cross gave them a very welcome present of tobacco and said that he hoped the two parties could join up in the near future.

Around Christmas time Barry and his party visited them again and told them something about their work. By January, 1942, it had become obvious to those in command in Malaya that the Japanese would inevitably capture the whole peninsula. Whether Singapore Island could be held for long was questionable, but few envisaged at that time quite how far the enemy would spread.

The rapid Japanese advance had precluded any plans to leave properly organized parties who would be able to fight behind the Japanese lines in conjunction with Chinese volunteer forces. Some groups were hurriedly cobbled together and put into the jungle, but these were ill-prepared for a long existence in enemy-occupied territory.

A few individuals, familiar with the jungle in peacetime, managed to survive the war, and some of the others displayed such courage and endurance that they too lived to tell the tale. But the majority were either betrayed to the Japanese or died in the jungle of malaria, beri-beri or malnutrition. In most cases those who survived lived with Chinese Communist guerrillas. Life with these fanatics often became very frustrating and many of the British felt that they were serving no useful purpose as far as the prosecution of the war was concerned and that they were, in fact, prisoners of the Chinese Communists instead of the Japanese. But the Chinese showed no hostility towards their inconvenient guests and even the most dedicated of them performed many acts of personal kindness. It is true to say that without the help of the Chinese, whether Communist or not, no British party could have survived the war, especially as their entry into the jungle had been so precipitate.

James Barry's group had a purpose and as much preparation as had been possible. Their orders were to operate a secret wireless station to areas still held by Allied forces once the Malay Peninsula had been overrun by the enemy. Their station, known as Station A, was to be situated in Johore in the mountainous jungle region of Gunong Blumut. From here it was intended to work to Station B on Singapore Island. If Singapore were to fall they would then work to Station Y in Java and, if that also were to be silenced, to Station R in Rangoon. In the event they worked only briefly to Station Y before wireless silence fell as the whole of South-East Asia came under Japanese domination.

Barry was a young Government official who had spent several years in the country and spoke perfect Malay. He had been engaged in counter-espionage on the Malay–Siam border before the Japanese invasion. Energetic and with a mercurial temperament, he was full of enthusiasm and charm. With hindsight, perhaps he was not a good choice for what turned out to be a long slog in the jungle, under the sometimes frustrating patronage of the Chinese Communists, and where he had little opportunity to exercise his volatile nature.

CQMS John Cross and Sergeants Morter and Wagstaff formed the Signals team which actually ran and operated the wireless station. Cross, in civilian life a Company Secretary, was aged thirty and was a much more mature and steady character than Barry. It was mainly his patient handling of the Chinese (so often upset by Barry's impetuosity) and his determination to avoid any form of friction among members of the group that enabled all but Barry to survive the many dangers and hardships which were to beset them during more than three years in the jungle.

Their entry, south of Kota Tinggi, at the end of January, 1942, was attended by the inevitable rush and chaos caused by the rapid approach of the Japanese. Nevertheless they had been able to purchase some suitable clothing, they had plenty of weapons and ammunition in addition to their wireless equipment, some European tinned food, medicines and maps – a total of some one hundred man-loads.

They were physically fit, apart from shortage of sleep over the past four hectic weeks, and had some knowledge of the country and its peoples. Their chances of survival were very good compared with those of soldiers who had been cut off, often wounded, knowing nothing of Malaya and with no maps, food or medicines and, in many cases, without weapons. But their real strength lay in the fact that they were in the care of Chinese guerrillas and guides from the moment they entered the jungle.

Even so, they had suffered many hardships, some illness and much danger from Japanese attacks, quite apart from the defection to the enemy of two of the guerrillas who knew of their location. They were hounded from one camp to another and had several narrow escapes from capture. After the second, Christmas meeting, another three months were to pass before the two groups joined up permanently, and by that time Barry's party had occupied fifteen different camps.

CHAPTER EIGHT

The Enemy Closes In

In January, 1944, there was great excitement as the Chinese brought in two soldiers who said they had escaped from Changi POW Camp on Singapore Island. These two, named Bill and Nick, said they were American aircrew, and Bill alleged that he was a member of the Communist Party of America.

They lived with the soldiers for several days and, at first, were welcomed as the four men pumped them for news of their comrades who were prisoners. Bill and Nick did not seem to know any of their friends, nor indeed much about POW life in Changi. They boasted about their escape and about what they proposed to do to the Japanese now that they were free to go and fight them; and they tried very hard to persuade the other four to leave the camp and go along too.

Jim and his companions soon became suspicious that these two had not escaped at all but had been deliberately infiltrated to the guerrillas by the Japanese. They decided to pass on their suspicions and one day when Bill and Nick were out of the way, Jim went to see the Committee. One of its members, 'Charlie', spoke good English and Jim was able to explain to him how they felt about the new arrivals. 'Charlie' promised to discuss the matter with the other Committee members, and later he went to see Barry and Cross, explaining that he also had had his suspicions because Bill, allegedly a member of the Communist Party of America, had been unable to name either its Chairman or its Secretary.

Then Barry and Cross met and talked to the newcomers and very quickly agreed with the general opinion that they were phoneys. Undoubtedly they were POWs and had spent some time in Changi, but they were obviously not Americans. They said that they had been shot down in Burma while with the US Cobra Squadron and had later been shipped to Singapore by the Japanese. But when questioned about the aircraft he had been flying Bill asserted that they were Swordfish, which were never flown by the Americans, in Burma or anywhere else; nor did a Cobra Squadron exist.

John Cross also noticed that Bill spoke his rather exaggerated American with a strong Birmingham accent. Whereas Bill was physically unattractive, Nick was suave, glib and good-looking. He spoke with a typical English Grammar School accent and was also fairly fluent in Malay. While a POW in Singapore he had, he said, been driving a lorry for a Japanese warrant officer and, reading between the lines, Cross suspected that he had formed a close attachment to this man and had, as a result, enjoyed a greater measure of freedom and better food than had his less fortunate comrades in Changi. It seemed likely that the two were extreme cases of what POWs called 'Jap happy'.

Another oddity was that, unaware that Barry and Cross received regular BBC news bulletins on their radio, Nick and Bill boasted about secret radio receivers in Changi and produced some astounding pieces of information which they said they had heard before their escape. They had no idea that Barry and Cross were able to check these snippets. There *were* secret radios in Changi, and in other camps. News was given out first to officers and then, after about a week, to the men. No amount of warnings would stop the men from careless talk in the presence of the Japanese, but by delaying news to them until it was 'cold' the danger to the wireless operators was greatly reduced.

Of course, Cross and Barry did not know about the receivers in the POW camps, but they *did* know the correct news; anything else produced by the newcomers as fact only confirmed suspicions that they had been living with the Japanese rather than with the other POWs. It was decided to watch them closely.

Their anxieties were increased by the news that the Japanese had located the camp and were closing in on them. Brian and Fred were both ill at the time, so it was Jim who went down with Douglas, a few days later, to the potato store by the Sungei

Tengkil bridge. While they were making up their loads the guerrillas suddenly started to panic as one of them had spotted a boatload of six Japanese coming up the river towards them.

The river here ran through a deep gorge. Douglas and Jim took two rifles from the Chinese, whom they persuaded to get under cover and keep quiet, and took up a position overlooking the river. As the Japanese paddled slowly into view, the two soldiers opened rapid fire and killed all the occupants of the boat. Then they handed back their smoking rifles. Though grinning with delight, the guerrillas begged the soldiers not to talk about it in camp or to say that they had had to do the shooting themselves. Douglas and Jim agreed, but there was no doubt in their minds that, had they not been there, the Chinese would have run off without firing a shot. Leaving some of them to make sure that the Japanese were all dead and to collect their weapons and ammunition, the two soldiers walked back to the camp.

With the enemy so near, food supplies were reduced to a trickle. Often they had only *kueh*, so the soldiers were surprised, a few evenings later, to be given an excellent meat stew. When they could eat no more, they went to congratulate the cooks and asked them what the delicious meat was, since there were no monkeys in the area.

'Orang Japun,' (Japanese men) the cooks replied.

Brian and Fred had both recovered, which was just as well, as it looked increasingly likely that they would soon have to leave the camp, and at short notice. Brian had brought a message to Jim from the guerrilla leader who had saved his life by rescuing him from the jungle in March, 1942. This man was now in the hospital; his legs had given way as a result of malnutrition and he was unable to walk. Jim resolved to go down to the hospital to see him, but before he could do so, events took a dangerous turn.

On 20 February a Japanese force surprised the jungle-edge sentry position and killed six guerrillas, the other five, some of them wounded, only just escaping with their lives. It was time to move.

On 3 March Barry's group, plus the armourer/blacksmith Ah Gui, moved to the new camp, their sixteenth, where they prepared huts for the others to join them a week later. It was a far better site than any of their previous camps; it was on high ground where the air was fresher and the nights less oppressive.

The remainder of the HQ, including the four soldiers and Nick and Bill, moved out also, walking up the stream by the cookhouse. They followed the stream for several miles so as to leave no tracks for the Japanese to pursue. When they left the stream the party split into two, Bill and Nick going off with some of the HQ guerrillas. Soon afterwards they all heard the sound of machine-gun fire in the vicinity of the camp which they had just left. It gave them some satisfaction to think of the Japanese making a strong attack on the empty huts, but they realized that they had only left in the nick of time.

Jim's party had a long march before camping in an empty house in open country, not far from Lenggui tin mine. Here they found some vegetables growing in the garden, and helped themselves.

Their security here was short-lived. At dawn the Japanese, perhaps informed by traitors of the movements of the HQ party, put in a surprise attack supported by heavy machine-gun fire. By a miracle no one was hit and they all dashed up a dried watercourse and into a swamp, where the Japanese lost them. The Chinese had become very panicky and most of them went off in a different direction, while the four soldiers and a few of the guerrillas plodded on through the swamp until they came to an established camp in which slit trenches had been dug. It rained hard all that night; the trenches filled with water and the whole place became a quagmire.

The following afternoon the Japanese burst yelling into the camp, taking the occupants by surprise. There was no time to escape so Jim, Brian and Fred seized rifles from the guerrillas, while Douglas Guest threw himself down behind a Bren gun and opened fire. This attack was beaten off but the Japanese quickly reorganized themselves and came in again, only to be thrown back after suffering heavy casualties.

Then enemy reinforcements arrived and the soldiers began to run short of ammunition. Douglas could only fire the Bren gun in short bursts. Suddenly Jim heard him call out, although he could not hear what he said because of the noise of the firing. At last he realized what Douglas was trying to tell him; lying terrified, close to Jim, was a guerrilla with two hand-grenades attached to his belt. They were enclosed in the usual *rattan* basket; Jim cut them free, but then found that he could not extract the pins as these too were covered with plaited *rattan*. Desperately fumbling with his knife, expecting the Japanese to overrun him at any moment, he at last cleared the *rattan* and released the pins.

He threw the grenades in the direction from which most of the enemy fire was coming, praying that they would not hit a tree and bounce back on him, and that they would explode. Luckily they both went off with a tremendous bang right on target, and the Japanese fire from that quarter was greatly reduced. The soldiers had often joked among themselves about the way the guerrillas carried their hand-grenades in these baskets; it seemed less funny now.

Shortly after the second attack darkness fell, and the defenders quietly slipped away into the swamp. All night they sloshed slowly along, and, just before dawn, heard gunfire in the distance and assumed that the now empty camp was being attacked again.

They kept on the move all that day and at night made some rough shelters in which to crouch, out of the continuous downpour of rain. Local civilians to whom the guerrillas spoke confirmed that there were a great many Japanese troops in the area and that they were making a determined effort to wipe out the British radio group and to disrupt the whole organization of the 4th Guerrilla Battalion. Was it coincidence, Jim wondered, that this big enemy operation followed so soon after the arrival of Bill and Nick?

Their guides said that they were taking them to join the radio party who were in a safe camp. Perhaps because they had lost face during the attack, the guerrillas asked the soldiers to say nothing about it. In spite of the shortage of food they had a good stew that night and suspected that again they were eating Japanese flesh. They preferred not to ask, and in any case it was that or nothing.

After five days of hard travelling they reached Barry and his men, and here they were to remain for the time being. That night they listened on the radio to the news from New Delhi. To this day Jim is carried back to those times whenever he hears the march tune which preceded these nightly news bulletins, which made them feel almost as if they were back in civilization. But the news from Burma was not good. The Japanese had mounted a massive attack against the Allied bases at Imphal and Kohima and were proclaiming that this was the start of 'the march on Delhi'. They were advancing on all fronts in Burma and were confident that they would drive the Allies out of India. This seemed to postpone indefinitely the return of British forces to South-East Asia, although the news that General Wingate had launched a second and bigger operation deep into Japanese-occupied Burma gave the listening exiles a faint glimmer of hope.

A day or two later the party with Bill and Nick arrived, bringing with them a small stock of emergency food. These two had become a problem which could no longer be ignored. Since the first Japanese attack they had been agitated and had acted strangely. They grumbled about living conditions in the jungle which were, they insisted, worse than at Changi. If they were asked what they wanted to do they always replied that they were longing to go out of the camp to fight the Japanese. It appeared to the others that, having been infiltrated to the guerrillas, they now had to find a way of escaping back to the Japanese and their only hope lay in defection during a brush with the enemy. They hung around the radio hut so that Cross had to cover up the wireless, and, in the cookhouse, kept pumping the four soldiers for information about the radio party.

The situation could not be allowed to continue, especially as the proximity of large forces of Japanese might at any moment give the traitors a chance to go over to the enemy. Barry, Cross and 'Charlie' had by now come to the firm conclusion that Bill and Nick had indeed been planted on them; it was decided therefore to pretend to agree to their requests for action by attaching them to a jungle-edge patrol.

A farewell party was given for them and then, much to the relief of the other British, they left the camp with a guerrilla patrol. John Cross felt sure that they would be executed by the Chinese, and indeed, if they were prepared to betray their own countrymen to the horrors of Japanese interrogation and torture, merely for their own selfish ends, then they deserved nothing but death. At the same time he could not help feeling sorry for them. By their clumsy spying and strange behaviour they had almost immediately aroused suspicion among both British and Chinese. They must have known this to some extent and yet were unable to get out of the situation in which they had landed themselves. Perhaps they knew that they were doomed men as they left the camp with the Chinese; at any rate, some time later 'Charlie' told Cross that Nick had died and was buried near Poh Lee Sen, and then that Bill had taken an overdose of medicine while he had fever and was dead too.

Near the camp were some old mine workings, a few of them flooded to a depth of twenty feet. As there was not much to do in the cookhouse because food was so scarce, Jim decided that he would learn to swim, an essential skill in this land of rivers but one he had never had an opportunity of learning. 'Waggy' (Sergeant Wagstaff) loaned Jim his leather belt to which Jim attached a long piece of *rattan*. Every day he practised until he could swim a few yards without sinking. About ten yards out from the bank there was a tall stake, and one day Douglas Guest swam out to this and called to Jim to join him. Jim had nearly reached the stake when he suddenly sank to the bottom of the pool. Spluttering and flailing his arms in terror, he at last surfaced and Douglas was able to grab him before he sank again. After that episode, Jim decided to be less ambitious.

Meanwhile Japanese forces were again getting close to them and before long they spent a very anxious twenty-four hours. Morter and Wagstaff had gone down with a party of Chinese to recharge the radio batteries on the diesel engine at the old HQ camp. While they were away Japanese planes attacked the civilians at the Tengkil mine with bombs and cannon fire. The inhabitants, lulled into a false sense of security by the apparent superiority of the guerrillas in the area over the past few years, were caught unawares and suffered many casualties. The British, hearing the bombardment, waited tensely; at last the two sergeants arrived back unhurt but with the batteries still uncharged.

After the bombing, reports came in that thirty lorry-loads of Japanese troops had left the main road and were converging on Tengkil on foot. The guerrilla patrols on the two approaches to Tengkil were completely outnumbered by Japanese infantry and fell back on the village. More Japanese poured in by another route which they had been secretly cutting through the jungle for weeks and the guerrillas only escaped from the trap by splitting up into small groups.

Worse was to come; a steady stream of civilian refugees took to the jungle tracks and unwittingly blazed a trail for the

Japanese towards the waterfall camp, where the occupants were quite unprepared for another move so soon after the previous one. Hurriedly they hid all the heavy gear and, with only an hour of daylight left, set off into the jungle where they hid uncomfortably during the night. Almost immediately the refugees began to catch up with them. This meant that the Japanese would probably soon follow, and might well have infiltrated collaborators among them.

It had become imperative to move again as the Japanese were closing in. They decided to break through trackless jungle for a time and to put a large hill between them and the approaching enemy so that no sounds such as woodcutting would give them away. This was achieved, and they hoped that they had finally thrown both Japanese and refugees off their trail. But the new camp was a cheerless place and brought back to the soldiers vivid memories of their time in the 'death shack' and other deep jungle camps. All around them the dripping vegetation pressed in close and the dark canopy overhead afforded no glimpse of sky. Soaked to the skin, and crowded into rough shelters of *atap*, the only way they could raise their spirits was by lighting fires of dead wood. There was no danger that the smoke would penetrate the dense foliage and give them away, and the fires did at least make it possible to dry their clothes.

Worse still, they had had to hide the radio so were without the tonic of news each evening; there seemed little likelihood that they would be able to recover it, or recharge the batteries, for the next month or two.

Food was minimal, consisting only of a small quantity of the unpalatable potato flour and a few small dried fish about the size of sardines. Half a coconut shell of this revolting mess twice a day left them always hungry but without any appetite for the next meal of this food which was so hard to swallow. They drank a great deal of boiled water which seemed to alleviate the pangs of hunger to some extent.

Within a week they were suffering from acute malnutrition which affected the Chinese as much as the British. Blurred vision and a weakness in the neck muscles, so that their heads lolled on to their chests or to one side, were the first symptoms. Jim found that he had to hold up his head with one hand when he wanted to eat. Then the paralysis spread to his stomach until he could not stand upright. There was no pain and sometimes the worst effects wore off, but they always returned later and at increasingly frequent intervals.

It seemed unlikely, however, that the Japanese would be able to supply their troops in deep jungle for very long, and sooner or later they would be forced to withdraw. But they had been successful in dispersing the guerrilla formations and now controlled every jungle path for miles around, so it was impossible for the radio party either to move or to bring in supplies until the Japanese had gone.

While they waited, the fugitives took stock of their surroundings and found there were plenty of *nibong* trees nearby. This palm has an edible heart, but Jim found it no easy matter to cut down the tree with one hand while holding up his head with the other.

Very soon the old claustrophobia and restlessness came back, to no one more acutely than Barry, who, out of the blue one day, told Cross that he intended to go off for a couple of months. He maintained that he could get the support of the Johore Malays, many of whose leaders had been his friends before the Japanese invasion. He even hoped that they might, in time, agree to cooperate with the Communist guerrillas. He would take the four soldiers and he asked Cross to let them have the Tommy gun and three rifles which he and the sergeants held. This left Brian unarmed, but these were all they had. In addition to trying to get Malay support, he said, he would attack a Japanese vehicle with a view to getting petrol and batteries and these he would send back to Cross with Chinese civilians so that the wireless station could be set up again. Finally, if all else failed and if the opportunities appeared good, he would try to get out of Malaya and link up with Allied forces elsewhere, and would then get in touch with Cross by wireless.

Cross, aware of the antipathy and distrust which existed between the two races, especially in relation to the Communist Chinese with their stated intention of taking over Malaya once the Japanese were driven out, thought that Barry was being far too optimistic, and that his plans were, in any case, unsound. To begin with, the loss of the weapons would leave the radio party defenceless; then again, Barry was proposing to leave without telling the Chinese, as he was afraid they would prevent him. This would immediately create distrust between the soldiers and the guerrillas. Barry was proposing to travel without guides, and there was every chance that the party, alien and armed, would be betrayed to the Japanese, who would either kill them out of hand, or torture them first and possibly extract the whereabouts of the radio party.

For all these reasons the plan seemed to Cross to be fool-hardy. And even if they were fortunate enough to fall in with other bands of guerrillas, there was no guarantee that they would be friendly; at the very least, they would probably relieve them of their weapons.

Cross put these points to Barry but the latter seemed deter-mined to go and so Cross had little option but to help him with his plans. He agreed to break the news to the sergeants, and Barry said that he would tackle the soldiers. Shortly afterwards he called them together, outlined his plans and said that he wanted them to come with him.

While Barry was talking, Jim became aware that the others were all looking at him, and he knew just what they were thinking. Could their constitutions stand any more prolonged hardships? And did Barry realize how hard life could be in the jungle, outside the protective envelope provided by the guerril-las? For the past two years he had been relatively well-fed and sheltered by the Chinese and had not had to endure the hardships which the soldiers had experienced and which had killed so many of them. Yet in spite of the easier time he had had, he did not seem to be as tough as they were. And supposing he were to be killed, or to fall ill and die, what would become of them, leaderless and adrift in strange country? They knew that he was a Political Officer who had been commissioned in the rank of Major overnight and that he had neither the basic training of an infantry officer nor any actual experience of jungle warfare. He was now setting himself, and them, a task which would have tried the capabilities of even highly-trained, fit and well-equipped forces. Would he, or they, be able to meet the challenge without even the help of the Chinese, or would the operation be doomed to failure at the outset?

After Barry had finished speaking, there was a long silence. Then they asked him if Lee Boon, Barry's interpreter and assistant, could come with them, but Barry vetoed this on the grounds that he would be sure to tell the guerrillas of their plan. The war was going to go on for a long time yet, he said, and it was up to them to do their bit for the Allied cause. Here they were both helpless and useless.

All of them, the two sergeants as much as the other four, had deep reservations, and Jim particularly disliked the idea of their sneaking off without a word to the Chinese. They had had much kindness from them, and this seemed a poor way of repaying it. And there were other objections, too. Without guides, relying solely on map and compass, there was a better than even chance of getting lost in this impossible country. And suppose Barry succeeded in making contact with his Malay friends? Some Malays had been very quick to hand British fugitives over to their Japanese masters – why should these be any different?

Yet none of the seven was able to formulate his reasons for disliking the idea, and eventually they agreed to go along with it, however reluctantly.

On 15 April they got together with the radio party and divided up the weapons and ammunition as well as their few possessions. They took some money, M & B tablets, binoculars, compass and maps, and a few pounds of oatmeal and potato flour. They had one *parang* and a saw for making shelters, and a few matches which Barry gave to Jim to carry and keep dry. On the following night they filled their water bottles and tried to get some sleep before setting out at dawn. During the night Barry was very restless, and Cross observed him prowling about and acting in a strange manner. He wondered whether Barry's mind was beginning to be affected by their precarious life.

Before dawn Cross woke them and they quickly got ready to leave. Jim said goodbye to the three remaining men of the radio party, wondering if he would ever see them again, and then the little group slipped noiselessly out into the darkness and vanished in the jungle.

CHAPTER NINE

Major Barry's Disastrous Expedition

Barry and his four companions skirted silently round the guerrillas' sentry posts without being detected. Soon the dawn came up and they pushed on quickly without meeting anyone. Rising for nearly thirteen hundred feet to the north-west lay Bukit Jengeli. The party climbed laboriously up through the dense jungle on its slopes until they reached the summit. Here the trees thinned out and Jim, taking the binoculars, climbed one of them. He could see the tin mines in the distance but there was no sign of life there.

Barry decided to follow a compass course due east, calculating that they would reach the Kota Tinggi–Mersing road within two days. They kept going until late afternoon and then made camp. During the journey they had come across many signs of wild life, including elephant tracks up to a foot deep in the mud, so there seemed to be no danger that the Japanese were patrolling this thick country.

After eating a meagre meal of *kueh* washed down with plenty of hot water, they sat round the fire drying out their clothes which were soaked with sweat. Barry outlined his plan again, and added that they must try to get in touch with Captains Davis and Broome and Major Chapman, all of whom, the guerrillas had told them, were operating in north Malaya.

Next morning, after a hurried meal, they rolled up their blankets and dry clothes in a groundsheet so that they could have some comfort on arriving at the next camp. By midday it was pouring with rain. The many small streams quickly became roaring torrents and the travellers constantly slipped and fell in the mud. Miserably they battled on over mountains, through swamps and across open ground. They skirted areas of thick jungle until they found gaps through which to pass. They had long ago learned that trying to slash a path, in the manner so often portrayed by Hollywood film directors, sapped their strength and produced very little result. In a head-on collision with the jungle, it was always the jungle that won.

At last, so weary that they could go no further, they stopped and lit a fire to dry themselves. They were far too tired to build a shelter and fell asleep round the fire as soon as they had eaten.

At breakfast they finished their supply of *kueh* and decided to keep the oatmeal as a last reserve because they hoped to reach the road that evening. But it was not to be. All day they struggled along a valley full of enormous boulders which made their progress slow and painful. Jim had an eerie feeling that this valley was haunted and hostile to their intrusion.

The next two days were the same; rain poured down on them continually and in the evenings they were too exhausted to build shelters. The oatmeal was soon finished and they only found one *nibong* tree to provide a scrap of nourishment.

After almost a week of this, the situation was desperate. They tottered along oblivious of their surroundings and conscious only of their aching limbs and failing strength. Then, at about midday, they were jolted out of their stupor by the sound of traffic. Jim was almost asleep on his feet and he realized what a great mistake they had made in trying to cross jungle country without the help of guides. Now they were exhausted and in no state to cope with any dangers which the road and human habitation might hold in store for them.

Heading cautiously towards the noise of the traffic they came out of the jungle at last on to a broad track. They estimated that they were within a few hundred yards of the road, so, hiding their gear in the undergrowth, they reconnoitred, keeping off the track but close to it. Presently they heard voices and saw that Chinese workmen were going to and fro along the track. At that moment a sounder of about twenty wild pig rushed past them, but they dared not shoot one until they knew more about the people here.

At last a Chinese *towkay* (a merchant), smartly dressed and wearing a white topee, came along. Barry and Brian stalked him while the others remained under cover. Half an hour later they returned and reported that there was a timber yard further up the track, in which many men were working with elephants. They had not seen any Japanese there.

They remained hidden until after dark and then crept down to some houses which lay on either side of the track where it joined the road. Douglas warily approached a house, while the others gave him cover. After a short interval he returned with a very frightened Chinese. Barry assured the man that they would not harm anyone and eventually he calmed down and went off to fetch them food and tobacco. Before going he advised them to be on their guard because the road was well-used by the Japanese, although less so at night for fear of guerrilla ambushes. He said that there were no Japanese living here but that they had strong forces at Kota Tinggi some fifteen miles to the south.

While the man was away getting their food, more Chinese, including women and children, came out of the houses to talk to them. Barry told them that the British would soon be back to drive out the Japanese. An elderly Chinese woman offered Jim her purse.

'*Saya tidak mahu terimakaseh*' ('I don't want it, thankyou') said Jim. Although they needed the money, he could not bear to take it from the old woman.

'*Saya faham*,' (I understand) she replied with a warm smile. This kind, spontaneous gesture from someone of another race touched Jim deeply.

The soldiers bought some sweet potatoes and tobacco and then went back to the place where they had concealed their gear. They had a smoke and chatted for a bit and then lay down and slept until dawn.

They woke much refreshed, apart from stiff limbs, and decided that this would be a good place to stay for a few days while they built up their strength. They went further back into the jungle and built a shack with wild banana leaves, which fortunately were plentiful here. They did not bother to make a sleeping platform, but spread a thick layer of the leaves on the ground.

When this was finished, Barry said that he wanted to watch the traffic on the road, so, carefully avoiding any houses, they made a detour through the jungle until they came to the road at the 47th milestone. Here they had an ideal position above a cutting so that they could look straight down into the passing vehicles. All day long traffic roared by, sometimes in convoy and sometimes as single trucks, many of which were being driven by British POWs under Japanese guards. Jim wondered if he knew any of them.

Barry said that they must ambush a single lorry or car, preferably late in the day when traffic had died down a little. He added that they must not smash it up as they needed the petrol and batteries, and anyway it might be driven by a POW. He asked Jim if he would be prepared to drive the captured vehicle along the road and up the track to the timber yard where they could strip it at leisure. But Jim pointed out that this was too close to the Chinese houses, whose occupants would assuredly be massacred in revenge, and he managed to persuade Barry to drop the idea. They returned to their shack, and Douglas shot a monkey which gave them a good meal that night.

They rested for the next three days, studying maps and making plans. Their maps showed a derelict narrow-gauge railway leading to the Middleton tin mines along the valley of the Sungei Kayu, and Barry thought they might be able to use this to get the petrol and batteries to the radio party. The Sungei Kayu joined a large river, Sedili Besar, at a point quite close to the road and about five miles south of their present position. Barry decided that this was where they should set up their ambush.

The following night they set off south. As they passed the shuttered houses a great many dogs began barking, which frayed the soldiers' nerves. They met no one on foot but occasionally lorries came along the road and they had to dive for cover. The undergrowth consisted largely of *mengkuang* with long stiff leaves like swords, covered with thorns, and soon they were all bleeding from many scratches. On the way they passed a potato patch and took the opportunity of filling their bundles.

It seemed a very long march, but at last they came to a place where the road ran through a cutting.

'This will do!' announced Barry. 'We can drag the branch of a tree across the road and force the driver to stop.'

But now that they had got down to planning the details of the ambush, they realized that they would need rubber tubing and cans for syphoning out the petrol. Nearby was an empty house, but a search of it revealed nothing suitable, nor was it likely that they would find such equipment lying about in the jungle.

'Very well,' said Barry, 'we must go back, and then tomorrow Fred and I will go to Kampong Danau and buy what we need.'

Wearily they retraced their steps as soon as it got dark. In the morning Fred and Barry left the others in hiding and set off, but they became hopelessly lost on the way and, although they eventually reached the *kampong*, they returned empty-handed two days later.

After a welcome meal of monkey which the others had cooked, Barry insisted that they should all go to Danau that night, in pouring rain, and they arrived before dawn in a rubber plantation where they made a fire to dry their clothes.

When it was light they visited the *kampong* and had some food. The Chinese there suffered badly from jungle ulcers in their legs, some of the holes being down to the bone, and they asked the party for medicine. Although they could ill afford to part with their precious M & B tablets, they felt that the Chinese were being helpful to them and deserved some help in their turn. So they gave them a few and showed them how to clean out the holes and put the powdered M & B into them.

The villagers, although friendly, were obviously anxious to get the British away from the *kampong* and they showed them a path to the Sedili River where, they said, the party would find a boat. The path led through a stinking swamp in which they sank up to their knees, and when they finally arrived at the river they found that the boat was far too small to carry all of them.

Barry and Brian swam a short distance up the river to a house on the far bank and here they found a larger *sampan* which the owner said they could have. It held them all but it leaked copiously and they had to take turns at baling it out. In this they cruised slowly down the river, which was very wide, uncomfortably aware that they were sitting ducks for any Japanese patrols on the banks, especially as the river ran close to the road in several places. They stopped for a meal and Jim managed to catch a few fish. By dusk they had come to a small bay not far from Lubok Pusing and here they tied up the *sampan* for the night.

In the morning they went ashore to talk to the inhabitants and to buy vegetables. The villagers were very keen for them to meet the local guerrillas, and presently some of these turned up.

They were carrying guns but, instead of coming forward to greet the British party, they took up firing positions behind the trees. The startled soldiers dived for cover and prepared to defend themselves, though they had no intention of firing the first shot. For a few minutes nobody moved; then Barry called across to the guerrillas that his party would go and get their gear and return for a conference in the morning. The Chinese made no attempt to stop them as they slipped away into the jungle and returned to the *sampan*. Under Barry's direction they set off back upstream, when they quickly found that paddling against the current was a very different matter from their easy ride down-river. On the way they passed what appeared to be swimming pythons over twenty feet long, which, seen almost from water-level, looked absolutely gigantic. Fortunately, none of them came near the boat.

At last they reached the empty house near the road where they had planned to have their ambush. Jim, to whom all these journeys to and fro over the same ground were beginning to seem like a bad dream, tried to persuade Barry to stop there. They knew that the local Chinese were friendly, and it was the best place they had yet found in which to waylay a Japanese vehicle.

But Barry had lost all interest in ambushes. He was convinced that the hostile guerrillas would follow and attack them and he was determined to get as far away as possible. So on they went, and at last they arrived back at the house where they had been given the *sampan* and returned it to its owner.

Here the Rivers Sedili and Ambat meet. They crossed the river on a high, rickety suspension bridge and set off in the direction of Bukit Petai, a hill nearly four hundred feet high and about three miles from the coast. They entered swampland and, after struggling into it until they felt that they could not be tracked, they found a dry place and cooked a meal. Afterwards they had a long discussion. In the end Barry decided that they should make for Jemaluang and Mersing.

'I know some influential Malays there,' he said, 'and they will be able to help us. But I wish now that I had taken your advice and brought Lee Boon with us as he might have been able to talk to those unfriendly guerrillas. However, we'll have to do the best we can and find a path to Jemaluang between the road and the sea.'

But the others could not help noticing that he seemed upset and worried. All his plans were going wrong and life was becoming very difficult.

The next day they struggled on through the swamp. Brian Smith had been struck by a severe attack of malaria and Jim's stomach was becoming weak again from malnutrition. Nor were the other three at all well. The going was very bad and they had to find roots to stand on to prevent themselves sinking in. Nowhere could they find the vestige of a path and it seemed as if the swamp would go on ahead of them for ever.

Worse still, they had finished all their food. Barry decided at last that they would have to make a detour to the east to Kuala Kambau in order to replenish their stocks. Kambau, according to the map, was not very far from the sea, and he thought that they might find a path from there to Jemaluang.

Before long they were completely lost. They found that they were going round in circles and when they stopped for the night they were absolutely drained of strength. They had nothing to eat and their matches were so wet that they could not even light a fire but just lay, soaking, cold and covered with leeches, on the wet ground.

For three more days they floundered on in the swamp. Fred Gooch, who carried the Tommy gun, a horrible weapon in close country as it was heavy and covered with knobs and levers, refused to let anyone else take a turn and bravely struggled along with his load. Barry had become silent and seemed utterly broken by the hardships, but they all knew that they had to keep going as the only alternative was death.

On the fourth day the ground gradually became less marshy and they began to look out for signs of habitation. Growing here were wild bananas and they noticed that some had recently been cut. After a time they came to a path which led to a hut. It was empty but inside were some children's dolls, so they felt sure that they could not be far from a *kampong*. The path went on to the jungle edge where they came up against a barbed wire fence. After getting through this they soon came into a *kampong*. It was Kambau, at last, with friendly Chinese who gave them a meal and sold them tobacco and potatoes.

But this ill-fated journey had again reduced them to a state of utter exhaustion. They craved rest, but Barry was adamant that they must push on without delay. Brian had not been able to shake off his malaria and at the thought of going on again he collapsed completely. Barry asked the Chinese if there were any guerrillas in the area and was told that the nearest were a long way away. He asked the villagers if they would look after Brian and, when his fever had passed, take him to the guerrillas, and they agreed.

At dawn next morning the soldiers said goodbye to Brian and set off along a track which the Chinese said would take them to Jemaluang. They did not like leaving Brian behind, alone and unarmed, particularly as he seemed past caring; but they had no alternative.

Jim had bought some matches from the villagers and they now had food and a path so at first things seemed to be looking up. But the track soon petered out and they found themselves back in the hated swamps. Douglas Guest went down with fever and Jim's head was lolling again and his stomach giving so much trouble that he had to stop frequently and then hurry to catch the others up. It was a terrible struggle but, at last, they stopped for the night.

That evening, Barry looked and acted very strangely and Jim had the worrying thought that perhaps their hardships and the failure of their mission were beginning to affect his mind. He had already been forced to leave Brian and now he could see that Jim was too exhausted to eat anything and that it was unlikely he would be able to go any further.

Next morning Barry told Jim to go back to Kambau and try to find the guerrillas when Brian was better. After some discussion Douglas said that he would go back too, partly because he himself had reached his limits but also because he did not think that Jim would ever reach Kambau alone. Barry and Fred decided to go on, Fred still insisting on carrying his awful Tommy gun. They divided up their possessions and shook hands. Jim and Douglas stood in silence and watched the others out of sight, admiring their sheer guts and hating to leave them, but Jim knew that he had given everything he had.

All day the two men struggled back towards Kambau, Jim collapsing frequently, and they did not reach the *kampong* until dusk. They called at the house where they had left Brian but he was not there. The Chinese told them that he had gone to join the guerrillas, but neither of them could believe that Brian would have recovered so quickly. They spent an uneasy night, the unpleasant thought that perhaps the Chinese had killed Brian returning to their minds again and again.

The following day they kept their rifles with them all the time and remained wary and watchful. Sure enough, while they were standing in some vegetable gardens about twenty armed guerrillas approached and spread out as if they were going to attack them. Douglas remarked mildly that they did not seem to be very friendly.

'This is it, then!' cried Jim, and they both jumped into some holes in the ground and prepared to die fighting.

'Let them fire first,' Douglas ordered. Tension rose as the guerrillas crawled behind the trees, but they did not shoot and seemed reluctant to come any closer. Jim wondered if the news had got round of how the British soldiers had used the guerrillas' weapons to kill the Japanese who had attacked them a short while ago, and he and Douglas were regarded as superhuman.

Whatever their reasons for holding back, it was clear to the two soldiers that the guerrillas had them trapped there, and that there was little chance of surviving if a battle started. Nothing happened. At last an old Chinese from the house where they had been fed came out into the open. He had been a cook on a P & O liner and spoke a little English.

'Come into my house. They will not shoot you if you give up your guns and then you can join your other comrade.'

Jim looked at Douglas. The guerrillas obviously dared not come near them while they were armed because they looked, and indeed were, desperate men. But if they gave up their rifles, anything might happen. However, they were cornered and really had no choice. Reluctantly they handed over their weapons and went into the house, where the guerrillas soon joined them. They still appeared hostile but did not touch the soldiers. After a little while they said that they would take them to join Brian.

After walking through the jungle for an hour or so they came to a derelict railway track. Here they stopped and were questioned by the guerrillas. Why had they left the 4th Guerrilla Regiment? Douglas replied that they were still British soldiers and had to obey the orders of their officers. One of the Chinese then came up to Jim and started to search him. He undid the top pocket of Jim's jacket in which he had his pay book, cigarette case and a few small possessions which he had managed to keep.

Jim flew at him and punched him on the jaw so hard that the man was knocked sprawling to the ground. Chattering with fury, he got up and pointed his rifle at Jim, who thought that this must surely be the end for him. But the other guerrillas restrained the man and no more searching was done.

After this unpleasant incident they continued their journey along the railway track, across some open country and through rubber plantations until, late in the afternoon, they came to a large house which had once been occupied by a British planter. There, to their immense relief, they found Brian unharmed.

They were given food and drink and a room in which to sleep. The guerrillas departed, leaving the three men with two Chinese, one smartly dressed and obviously important, who was hostile to them, and his servant who was friendly and helpful.

Late the following day, to the soldiers' astonishment, the guerrillas came back escorting Barry and Fred Gooch. They also had been disarmed and were so tired that they were unable to speak. At least, Jim thought, they were all together again, although without a weapon between them.

After a few days' rest, the discussions began. Barry was taking the fiasco into which his expedition had deteriorated very hard. Likeable though he was, he had the kind of character that is quickly knocked back by failure, and he lacked the resilience which the others either had naturally or had acquired. They acknowledged his courage, his determination to get to grips with the enemy and his frustration at two years of inaction but they also realized his lack of experience. What they did not understand was the irreversibility of his present depression. He was, literally, a broken man.

CHAPTER TEN

Out of the Valley of the Shadow

About a week later, in mid-May, a guerrilla leader came to see the soldiers. He had decided that it would be dangerous to keep them at the planter's house any longer and he made them set off with him at once. They walked all day in a north-easterly direction through patches of jungle and swamp, finally arriving at a shack which stood in open country and had some cultivated land round it. The Chinese gave them cooking pots, an axe and a *changkul* and told them how to grow vegetables and tobacco. He implied that no more food would be brought to them and that they would have to become self-supporting. The soldiers accepted this philosophically; after all they had left the 4th Guerrillas without permission and now they had to pay the price.

They were all fit again after their rest and Fred Gooch, a former farm worker, set to work at once on the garden. The others helped him clear the plot and set sweet potatoes by planting small pieces of the tops in the soil. They also planted *ubi kayu* and tobacco. Jim augmented their rations by fishing. He found holes in the swamps where there were fish and caught several, but some species had very sharp spines and as all scratches soon turned septic they had to be careful how they handled them.

Because the swamps were so close, the mosquitoes were terrible, worse than they had ever known, and the shack was thick with them every night. Although they lit fires and slept in the smoke this did not prevent the mosquitoes from making their nights miserable. By day it was extremely hot and they soon became very sunburned. But the heat brought on their malaria, too, and every day one or other of them was seized with uncontrollable shaking and lay shivering under his blanket until the fever broke.

Early in June they were moved again, this time back past their first house and then east into rubber plantations where there was another planter's house. The guerrillas had several huts here and they supplied the soldiers with food, so the latter assumed that they had served their term of punishment and that their gardening days were over.

At the end of June they were uprooted again and put in a strip of jungle in another rubber plantation. By now their health had deteriorated considerably and they were all laid low with malaria most of the time. However, they were only a few miles from the sea here and the Chinese often brought them a welcome ration of fresh fish.

Nevertheless, ill-health was having an increasingly depressing effect on their spirits, and no one was affected as badly as Barry. The four soldiers had been through so much together that they formed a very close-knit group, which may have exaggerated in Barry's mind the inevitable isolation of command. Whatever the reason, he grew more and more silent and withdrawn and the others became increasingly apprehensive about him.

Then one day at dusk he was missing from the hut. They went out and searched for him until it was too dark to see and then spent a wretched night wondering where he could have gone. At daybreak they resumed the search and soon came upon his body in some undergrowth. He had taken the cut-throat razor which they used for shaving and had opened the veins in his wrists.

They were all stunned. They knew that he had been in low spirits but had never suspected that he had reached the point where he would kill himself.

Jim reported Barry's suicide to the guerrillas who expressed genuine regret and helped to dig a grave for him. They even found from somewhere a Union Jack in which to wrap his body. It was possible that they felt slightly guilty because they had kept the British in such poor circumstances since they had disarmed them and were now trying to make belated amends.

The soldiers were very sad that one of their number had actually died, after so many narrow escapes. They missed

Barry even though he had not been very good company during
the past few weeks. In their eyes he was a good officer, with
plenty of courage, who had done his best for his country but
who had at last been defeated by illness and failure. Now,
unarmed and leaderless, they thought with nostalgia of their
happy days at Tengkil with Cross and the Chinese who were
their friends, and wondered if they would ever see them again.

It was only a matter of days before Douglas became very ill
with fever, often slipping into a raving delirium. To his horror
Jim saw in Douglas symptoms of the same fever which had
killed the Australians, Bill and Alan, in the 'death shack'.
Taking some of Barry's money he and Brian went to a *kampong*
some two miles away and tried to buy some medicine, but they
were told that the Japanese had taken all the quinine for their
own use, or perhaps to deny it to the guerrillas. All Jim was able
to buy for Douglas was a large bunch of bananas.

But by now Douglas was too ill to eat them. His body had
become so covered in bed-sores that they had to take off his
clothes. Feeling utterly helpless and in despair they sat by him
doing anything they could to ease his pain. But at last he lapsed
into unconsciousness. He lingered in this state for five days and
finally died on 13 July.

They buried him beside Barry and sat in their shack feeling
utterly miserable and numbed by despair. Jim had had a great
admiration for Douglas, and he had been through so much with
him that now he felt as if, with Douglas's death, something in
himself had also died.

Hardly had they buried Douglas than Fred Gooch began to
show the same symptoms. Brian Smith wrote a letter to John
Cross, telling him of Barry's suicide, Douglas's death and
Fred's fever. He asked Cross to try and get them back to his
party before they all died, especially as the guerrillas here were
not as friendly as those at 4th Guerrilla HQ. He gave the note to
the Chinese who promised to deliver it; they did not mention
that Barry, unknown to his companions, had already written to
Cross just before his suicide, saying that he was dying of an
unknown fever and only had hours to live.

Fred went rapidly downhill; he could not recognize his
friends and lost all control of his limbs. For a few more days he
lingered on and then he too died and was buried.

The deaths of these three, two of them old friends, shook Jim badly. There was a relentlessness about it, as, one after the other, his companions had been picked off, until only he and Brian remained. What hope had they of surviving in this savage place?

For a few days they simply sat about, too wretched to do anything, and forced by their circumstances into a closeness which lacked the spontaneity which had come naturally to the others. Brian was much younger, and, having lived all his life in the Far East, knew England only by hearsay. He was tough, however, beyond his years, and in this extremity of peril they had no option but to stick together. The prospect before them was grim in the extreme; but though they both knew it, they could not discuss it. In a sense, there was nothing to say.

After a while they came to the cold realization that their only hope was to write off the dead and look to their own survival. They walked to the *kampong* where Jim had tried to buy quinine. There was a coffee-house where the villagers congregated, and Jim and Brian spent many hours there, talking to them. It never ceased to amaze Jim that the Chinese did not seem to think it unusual that British soldiers should be in their *kampongs* in a country which had been occupied by the Japanese for nearly three years. They remained truly inscrutable in the traditional manner, and they reminded Jim of the old Norfolk saying, 'If yer doon say narthen, yer doon git wrong.'

The Japanese had been close at times in the past, and occasionally Jim saw trees that had been heavily scarred by bullets, but they had not troubled the guerrillas recently and there was an unaccustomed air of relaxation.

Jim and Brian made several trips to the coffee-house and also visited their garden where they found that the crops were growing well and they were able to pick some tobacco. Looking at the garden Jim felt a wave of misery passing over him; tears filled his eyes as he pictured Fred Gooch tilling the plot while they planted their vegetables. That vivid sense of loss was to stay with him for years; but now life was too precarious to allow for much brooding.

One day 'Big Jaw', the Hailam officer from Rengam whom they had known so well at Tengkil, came to see them. The news of the deaths of the other three seemed to affect him deeply, and when Jim asked him if they could rejoin Cross's party, he promised to try and arrange it. This meeting did much to raise their spirits and gave them the strength to hang on for a little longer.

In the big planter's house to which they had first come lived an elderly member of the Malayan Communist Party (MCP). One day Jim saw Brian talking to him and strolled over to see what was going on. The Chinese had an old twelve-bore shot-gun and some home-made cartridges. He wanted the two soldiers to shoot some monkeys which were numerous in a nearby part of the jungle. Brian told him that Jim was good with a gun, so the man gave it to Jim and said, 'You shoot'. They went off into the jungle, where Jim fired three shots and killed two monkeys which delighted the old man. But within minutes the place was swarming with armed guerrillas who, hearing the shots, thought that a Japanese patrol had arrived. They were so relieved to find who was shooting that they did not admonish Jim. Taking the monkeys back to the camp, they all had a good meal that evening.

Jim was feeling a lot better by now and, living in this open country, he had become as brown as any native. One day he overheard two Chinese talking about him. '*T'hee wrun,*' (He is an iron man) they said. They did not know that Jim understood quite a bit of Mandarin Chinese, and the remark pleased him enormously.

But now a new worry plagued his mind. Brian was suffering from increasingly frequent and severe attacks of malaria and seemed to be getting steadily weaker. As he nursed him, Jim watched anxiously for symptoms of the fever which had so recently killed the others. He tried to shut out of his mind the ghastly picture of Brian dying and himself being left alone.

Towards the end of July the guerrillas came and said that they were going down to the sea to capture a boatload of rice whose movements had been reported to them by their spies. They asked Jim to come with them as they knew that he was a good shot and there was a chance that the Japanese might arrive by sea and try to prevent the loss of the rice boat. Jim was none too happy about leaving the sick Brian, even for a few hours, but the guerrillas were very pressing and finally he agreed to go. They gave him a rifle and some ammunition and he followed them down a track which led to the sea, some three miles away, but he was firmly resolved not to indulge in any heroics on their behalf.

When they reached the shore some of the guerrillas embarked in small boats and paddled out to sea while the rest waited near the estuary of the Sungei Paloi. Presently there was a good deal of shooting and shouting in the distance and then the sea-going party reappeared with their prize, an old junk loaded with rice and crewed by twelve Siamese seamen. There was no sign of any Japanese so, leaving most of the guerrillas to unload the junk, Jim returned to camp, helping to guard the Siamese crew who were taken back there. The latter were sullen and refused to speak to the Chinese.

Jim had not tasted rice for over two years and it was a real treat. After only a few meals of it, he could feel his strength returning. In order to house the Siamese, Jim and Brian had to move to another hut. The wretched seamen were already becoming ill and some looked as if they would die before long. The first day in their new hut Brian had a fright. Lying fever-ridden on the sleeping platform he did not notice a twelve-foot-long black snake which had slithered in below him. Suddenly a vast reptilian head came up between the bamboo slats on which he was lying. Leaping up with a shriek, he called the Chinese who came running and soon killed the snake. They expressed disappointment that it had not been a coloured python as black snakes were considered inedible. (In fact, all snakes are edible and normally the Chinese will eat anything, black snakes included, so this must have been a local superstition.) Brian had no strong views about its colour, he just knew that he did not want to share his bed with any snake.

By early August Brian had recovered considerably and he and Jim received electrifying news. 'Big Jaw' arrived in camp and came to see them, friendly and smiling. He said he would take them back to join Cross and that they would start the following morning. The soldiers were jubilant, their only anxiety being about the journey itself: they had not forgotten making it in reverse with Barry and the going had been tough.

Early next morning they set off, 'Big Jaw' leading at such a spanking pace that they had a job to keep up with him. They travelled on good paths in open country and they realized more and more how foolish Barry had been to try and cross jungle country by compass course instead of using Chinese guides. They had all worn themselves out unnecessarily. This bitter thought kept recurring to them as they walked swiftly along good tracks instead of floundering waist-deep in stinking swamps.

In the evening they arrived at a hill camp situated, with the guerrillas' customary cunning, on a ledge with only one approach. There was a fighting patrol based here, some of whom were known to Brian and Jim. Among them was the barber who had been at 4th Guerrilla HQ and before they had their meal he trimmed their hair and made them look slightly less wild and jungly.

They went off again at dawn. For much of the day they walked on a path which ran through tall elephant grass and they could see nothing around them. In the evening they came to a house and 'Big Jaw' said, '*Berhenti di sini*' (Stop here). Jim noticed that he always spoke to them in Malay but he was sure that he understood English, so they were very careful about what they said to each other in his hearing. Jim had previously found that many of the guerrilla officers followed this line, presumably so that they could overhear discussions in English and thereby gain information.

During the night the Chinese woke them, saying that it was time to leave. Nearby was a small landing stage where they got into a boat which some civilians paddled downstream. Jim found it strangely frightening, in spite of his long acquaintance with the jungle at night, as they paddled down the black flowing river while the bushes on either bank, lit up by myriads of fireflies, twinkled like decorated Christmas trees.

A few hours later they came to the junction of the Sungei Kayu and Sedili where there was a big bridge which formed part of the Kota Tinggi–Mersing road. Before reaching the bridge they disembarked and made a detour through some swamps. As they reached the road a lorry came by, its head-lights sweeping the jungle, and they had to take cover behind a tree. When it was quiet again, they slipped silently across the road and entered the jungle on the other side. Close by was a civilian house where they were given a meal.

They pushed on again in the darkness and by dawn had reached a narrow-gauge mining railway which led to Middle-ton tin mines. Jim remembered that this was the route by which Barry had hoped to get petrol and batteries to Cross, had the ambush plan been carried out. They passed several small platforms which served as stations, but did not stop to rest as 'Big Jaw' was leading them at his usual furious pace.

At last they came to Middleton tin mines where the sun, reflecting up from the white sand, made them screw up their eyes which had been so long accustomed to looking only at the restful green of the jungle. They had a hurried meal in a house at the mine and then went on into the village. 'Big Jaw' left them to rest here while he went off to conduct some other business. The people here were strange, thought Jim; they took no notice of the two Englishmen at all. It was almost as if he and Brian were invisible to them.

Before long 'Big Jaw' returned and took them through the village and on to a camp in a small strip of jungle on a hill. The camp was empty but there was a supply of ready-cooked food for the night patrols there, so Jim and Brian had another meal after he had left them. At dawn he collected them again and they went on until they came to a village near Lenggui tin mine. Once more they walked along a railway track to a hut on the bank of the Sungei Lenggui. This was occupied by three middle-aged Chinese, one of whom had a wooden leg and was known to Cross's party as 'Peg Leg'. This was, in fact, a staging post for guerrilla couriers and other travellers and so far the Japanese had found nothing to connect it with the guerrillas so had let the three Chinese continue to live there. When Jim and Brian arrived to spend the night there were about thirty people, both civilians and guerrillas, lying on the floor of the hut.

The following morning they embarked in a *sampan* which the Chinese poled up-river. Every so often they had to lift the boat out of the water and carry it because fallen trees were blocking the channel. Jim thought that these trees had probably been felled deliberately to hinder Japanese boat patrols.

They were now just below Bukit Tengkil; a few miles away Jim could see Bukit Jengeli and he remembered the first day out with Barry when they had all five climbed to the summit. That was four long months ago, and he was still thinking about all that had happened since when the *sampan* drew in to a jetty and he saw John Cross, Morter and Wagstaff waiting to greet them.

As Jim jumped ashore Cross grasped his hand and said how pleased they all were to have him and Brian back again. Jim's heart was too full for words; it was as if he had come home and he could have hugged the owners of those smiling and welcoming faces.

That night they had a celebratory meal. The Sakai with whom Cross's party were living had caught a bear in a trap. Because their visits to the trap were infrequent, the bear had been dead some time when they found it, and gave off a sickening stench. However, they could not afford to waste good meat, and after a very unpleasant butchering job they cooked it with plenty of chillis. To their surprise the smell disappeared and the meat was delicious.

Afterwards they sat and smoked while Jim and Brian told the full harrowing story of their experiences since they had set out with Barry. As the tale unfolded, a deep sadness filled them all. Pessimistic as Cross had been about the expedition, the outcome was far more disastrous than he had ever imagined. But for Jim the loss of Douglas and Fred had a deeper, more tragic significance. From this time he turned more and more within himself, numbed by an overwhelming sense of hopelessness and fear which he would only slowly, and never entirely, shake off.

CHAPTER ELEVEN

John Cross's Story

After Jim and Brian had finished their account, Cross told them all that had happened since they left.

First he had the difficult task of breaking the news of their departure to the Chinese. Barry had given him a letter saying that he was taking the soldiers away on a special mission and apologizing for not having taken Cross into his confidence. He had thought that if Cross showed it to the guerrillas he would be absolved from any complicity. However, after consulting the two sergeants, Cross decided not to use the letter. He felt that if the Chinese accepted it they would think him very dim not to have noticed any preparations, and if they did not, the trust which he had been at such pains to establish would be instantly lost.

He gave the party as long as possible to get clean away, and when it became obvious that they would soon be missed, he sent for Ta (Big) Yu and told him that Barry and the soldiers had gone. Ta Yu was dumbfounded and went to consult 'Charlie', but neither of them knew how to handle it. John Cross then gave Ta Yu a formal letter to Central HQ asking for a meeting at which he would make a full statement. This pleased the two guerrilla leaders who felt that the matter was thus being taken out of their hands, especially as Cross reminded them that his party had originally been under the direct control of Central and only lived with the 4th Guerrillas for safety and convenience.

But they were still worried that Barry's party might be captured and, after torture, be forced to lead the Japanese to the camp. So they had it burned down, and led everybody back to what remained of the waterfall camp.

It was an agonising march; they were all suffering from the effects of malnutrition and stumbled along with their heads lolling grotesquely and their sight so blurred that they could hardly see where they were putting their feet. Cross was filled with foreboding about the future of Barry's party, equally debilitated, as he reached the camp and wearily helped in the putting up of shelters for the night.

They waited there for two days while Cross's letter to Central HQ was copied and sent off by two different routes. Neither runner got through; one met Japanese troops at Tengkil and swallowed his message, the other reached the last known location of the HQ only to find it deserted.

It was then that Cheong Khuen had a bright idea. When he had worked on the engines at Tengkil he had often met people of the aboriginal Sakai tribes who had come down from their jungle homes to sell fish which they had caught in the rivers. He knew that they lived up-river from Tengkil and was confident that he could find their *kampong*. He estimated that it was about half a day's march away across country where they would be unlikely to meet any Japanese.

After the failure of the runners to find HQ, Ta Yu felt free to act on his own initiative, and he liked Cheong Khuen's suggestion. Accordingly they all set off one morning and reached the Sakai *kampong* by noon. Here they received a warm welcome and were soon installed in a group of empty huts beside the river. The Sakai were so terrified of the Japanese that they had moved further into the jungle and built themselves new huts; even in the old ones, Cross's party and the guerrillas felt safer than they had done for two months.

The Sakai were a people of great charm and Cross often walked with them through the jungle and watched them climbing trees, at which they were expert. He carried no arms as he felt sure that their highly developed jungle senses would alert him to the approach of Japanese long before they came close enough to be dangerous.

As soon as they were settled in the *kampong*, the guerrillas tried again to get a message through to HQ. This time they succeeded and in due course a representative arrived. It was an old friend, Ah Ti, who had been promoted to Committee rank.

Barry had left two notes for Central HQ: one of them simply stating that he was leaving on an operation and that John Cross would be in charge of the radio station and all intelligence matters during his absence; the other setting out his reasons for going to get petrol and batteries and asking the guerrillas not to interfere. 'Charlie' translated the letters to Ah Ti who sat listening with an impassive face. He refuted the implication that the guerrillas were unable to get petrol for the generator, saying that they had captured four large drums, but, as these were a long way off, it would take time to get them to the camp. In fact, they never arrived.

Then Ah Ti expressed the usual worry that Barry's party might surrender to the Japanese, and when Cross assured him that they would not, he said that a group of Europeans would be much too conspicuous to get far, or to get help, and that as they were armed they might find themselves in trouble with hostile guerrillas from other areas.

Cross decided that it was time to go on to the offensive and he raised the question of the authority of 4th Independent HQ over the British party which had originally been set up under the direct control of Central. He also asked for some weapons to replace those which Barry had taken, but here he was on weaker ground and Ah Ti said that he had no arms to spare. However, he agreed that they could borrow rifles from the pool when out of camp or on a journey.

The discussion then became more general and several useful decisions were made. Ta Yu and Ta Ching and 'Charlie' Chai Chieh were to be the local directing party with the British. Ah Ti agreed there should be better consultation in future and asked them to prepare a weekly newsletter for despatch to Central every Monday. If the newsletter could go to Central, so, thought Cross, could a letter from him, in addition to those Barry had written. He was particularly anxious to get in touch with Captains Davis and Broome and Major Chapman who, according to the guerrillas, were operating further north. So far all his requests for contact had been ignored. He quickly wrote a letter to them and a note to Central HQ asking them to forward it. Ah Ti agreed to deliver the package and left in high good humour. Cross felt that trust, over which Barry's operation had cast a shadow, had now been reaffirmed between them.

On 8 May they produced their first newspaper since the Japanese attacks against Tengkil in March had closed down publication. News, coming in regularly now, raised their spirits, and life with the Sakai turned out to be very pleasant and harmonious, especially, it must be said, since the volatile Barry was not there. Even the Chinese seemed more relaxed and friendly, and there was plenty of time to bathe and to make river trips in the sampans. Food was plentiful; indeed, one day Cheong Khuen stumbled on two bears which were feeding on two wild pigs they had killed. In his fright he had fired his rifle, luckily driving the bears away, and everybody had a good feast on pork.

Relations with the Sakai were excellent and they decided to invite them to a concert party. The Sakai asked them back a few evenings later and 'Waggy' fixed up electric light under which the tribe did one of their dances, becoming more and more abandoned until they started to tear off their clothes. At this point 'Waggy' switched off the lights, fearing that their easy friendship with the Sakai might be endangered if the latter had remembered, in the sober light of dawn, that the British had seen their women dancing around stark naked!

Then, without warning, Cross himself became very ill with malaria. Morter and 'Waggy' carried on the routine work and nursed him devotedly and in the end he managed to shake it off, though it left him very weak.

Towards the end of May they began to have trouble with the generator. Cheong Khuen managed to get an old petrol/paraffin compressor engine from the tin mine but, as they had no paraffin for it, they had to run it on diesel fuel. The engine would not stand this for long and soon packed up, which meant that they would no longer be able to monitor news bulletins once their batteries had run down, and the newspaper would cease to be produced. They decided that they must recover their original charging engine and spare petrol from the ninth and eleventh camps where they had been hidden. 'Waggy' set out with five Chinese and three days later arrived back safely with the equipment. They quickly charged up all batteries as great things were afoot in Europe and they felt sure that the second front would start at any moment. By 16 June, knowing that the invasion of France had been successful, they were able to produce a newspaper giving the details.

And then Cross went down with another bad attack of fever. Although his inclination was to lie and do nothing, he remembered what had happened to the soldiers in the 'death shack', and how Jim had kept on walking about, and had survived. So each day he walked slowly round the clearing, until he found that what had at first seemed impossible was gradually becoming easier.

But he was getting weaker as he could not face the camp food. 'Charlie' was very worried about him and decided to send him down to the Chinese guerrilla hospital. With two Chinese guides the Sakai took him by boat to 'Peg Leg's' riverside house. This was as far as they dared go and for the rest of the journey he was pushed on a trolley by the Chinese along the railway line until they came to the transit camp with the big house (where Brian and Jim were to spend a night on their return to Cross). It so happened that one of the residents at that time was Johnny Long, a chemist's dispenser who had fled to the jungle rather than live under the Japanese. He had some phials of Australian quinine and he volunteered to look after Cross and treat him with these, to spare him any more travelling.

By the end of a week the patient had recovered sufficiently to make the journey back to his Sakai camp, spending a night with 'Peg Leg' on the way. On arrival he found an effusive, although non-committal, letter and some presents which had come from the South Johore Local Committee of the MCP; but there was no reply from the British officers to whom he had written. He repeated the letter and sent it off to Central by runner.

Meanwhile they were busy receiving BBC and American bulletins on the progress of the war, and after they had rigged up a loudspeaker they gave a news broadcast every evening, which even the Sakai attended.

Then, out of the blue had come Brian Smith's letter reporting the deaths of Barry and Douglas and asking Cross to try and get the rest of them back to his party. It gave him few details but Cross managed to extract from 'Charlie' the information that Barry had committed suicide.

He realized from the tone of Brian's letter that the three survivors were in a bad way and that unless some action could be taken quickly they might all die before long. He wrote at once to Ah Ti at HQ asking for the return of the soldiers and received a favourable reply a week later. Then he wrote to Brian saying that as soon as they were fit to travel they would be brought back to join him. Time was obviously vital, but all he could do was wait helplessly and hope that rescue would not arrive too late.

Cross could get no more information from the guerrillas as to why Barry had killed himself or why Douglas had died, until 'Charlie' handed him Barry's watch, fountain pen and spectacles and his note.

A silence fell over the listeners by the fire. Each man sat thinking his own thoughts about the tragedy and waste that had been revealed. Barry's suicide had deeply shocked them. His restlessness and frequent changes of mood had often irritated them, but his death brought home to them how much he had hated the pattern of their lives, his volatile spirit caged by the unremitting struggle for survival.

Now he was dead, partly a victim of his own character; it was a sad end for a young man of twenty-nine. Jim wondered miserably whether, with his long experience of survival, he might have been able to influence Barry if he had spoken out at the beginning against his plan. But it was too late now, and they were not out of the jungle yet.

CHAPTER TWELVE

Back in Touch

Cross brought Jim and Brian up-to-date with the progress of the war during their four months absence. In Burma the much-vaunted 'march on Delhi' had failed. The Japanese had hurled themselves repeatedly at the Imphal and Kohima defences in suicidal attacks but had been unable to capture them. At last, deprived by the failure of the Allied supplies on which they had counted, and with their own pitifully inadequate supply system in disarray, the survivors began to withdraw, leaving fifty thousand of their dead on the battlefield. Starving, riddled with malaria and dysentery, this broken army crawled slowly south, losing thousands more from malnutrition and disease during the retreat. The victorious 14th Army hunted them down and hurled the bedraggled remnants across the Chindwin River. It was the first major defeat of Japanese land forces and one from which they were not to recover.

In the Pacific the Americans were nearing the Philippines and British naval air attacks were being made on Sumatra. But the main news came from Europe. On 6 June the Allies had invaded France and, after several weeks of fierce fighting, were advancing rapidly. In the east, the Russians had driven the Germans from their soil and were now approaching Warsaw.

This was the sort of news that the little group by the river had been waiting for, and it worked on them like a tonic. 'Charlie' interrogated Jim and Brian, asking them again why they had left on Barry's expedition. Their departure was something which the guerrillas seemed unable to understand and of which they were automatically suspicious, as defection was usually a prelude to betrayal to the Japanese. The two soldiers repeated that they were still in the British Army and had to obey an officer's commands. In the end 'Charlie' seemed to be satisfied with this simple explanation and his attitude to them became as friendly as it had been in the past.

The Japanese were now threatening them again. Although enemy numbers had been reduced since their operations in March and April, they had retained considerable forces in the Tengkil area and most of the houses had been abandoned by their owners. This had led to pilfering by those who remained. 'Peg Leg' had foolishly left his riverside sanctuary and gone down to Tengkil to do a bit of looting. Loaded with his booty he was returning home when he was surprised by a Japanese patrol, and they were easily able to shoot and kill him. Knowing where he lived, the patrol had gone to his house, just missing his two companions who fled as the Japanese approached. This valuable staging post was thus lost to the guerrillas.

This setback was followed by an incident between a guerrilla courier and two Sakai who were guiding him back to camp. Having heard from local Chinese that enemy troops were close at hand, the guerrilla had pressed the Sakai, who were already exhausted, to push on faster. This they resented and slashed at him with a *parang* before bolting off into the jungle with his rifle. The wounded courier managed to struggle back to camp and, after three days in the jungle, hunger drove the two Sakai back also. An uneasy atmosphere settled on the camp as the tribe waited for the retribution which they expected.

Finally, unable to bear the suspense any longer, the whole tribe decamped in the night, leaving only the body of their elderly and dotty headman who had been unfit to travel. They had cut his throat and covered him with a sheet, with food and water to feed his spirit on its journey. It was unfortunate that the Sakai had decided to leave as they were a good insurance against surprise Japanese attacks and, had they but known it, 'Charlie' had not intended to do more than voice his disapproval of the conduct of the two guides.

In view of their departure, 'Charlie' decided that the party must move again. They went upstream by *sampan* and disembarked on the west side of the river where the Sakai had made a clearing of about three acres. From here they marched for several hours until they came again to the river, which they then recrossed to the east side. Here the guerrillas put up a few huts. But it was a miserable place, dank and sunless and swarming with leeches and mosquitoes.

Apart from Sergeant Morter, who seemed immune, they all started having attacks of malaria again and their food was reduced to *kueh* and water. Jim, remembering how they had kept alive by eating rats in the 'death shack', made a trap out of a biscuit tin. He caught one rat which he and Brian cooked and ate, and the disgust with which the others watched told him more clearly than any words that they had never known real starvation.

But they desperately needed meat. They could hear monkeys in the trees not far away, so Jim asked 'Charlie' if he could take a rifle and try to kill one. 'Charlie' agreed that it would be worth the risk of firing a shot and supplied him with a gun and ammunition. For several days Jim stalked his quarry without success; the monkeys were very wild and wary, possibly because the Sakai had hunted them in the past. In the end he crossed the river and found a large party of monkeys. He brought down a big one but when he went to pick it up he found a baby hanging on to its mother's body. Jim knew that it would not survive alone in the jungle so he was forced to kill it too. That night he and his companions ate well.

Flushed with his success, Jim went off again the following day to the same place, but the monkeys kept leading him on without giving him a chance to get a shot. Suddenly he realized that he had gone further than he had intended and that the light was fading. It was essential to get back to camp before dark, but he was not unduly anxious because he knew from experience that he only had to return to the river and follow it downstream.

He cast urgently about, following numerous Sakai paths, but nowhere could he find the river. He was utterly lost. Panic gripped him, but he fought it back. He must keep cool, think, act as his father would if he found himself in such a spot. He stood still, shouted, listened for a reply. No reply came. All was silent except for the jungle dripping and rustling round him. It was now almost dark and, to make matters worse, he began to shake with the onset of an attack of malaria. Guessing that the others would realize he was lost and would be listening, he decided to fire two shots, with a short interval between them, so that they could pick up the direction of his present position. The sound seemed to fill the jungle, but when the echoes had died,

there was only the same restless silence and the unbroken
darkness.

Then he heard a shout. Imagination? Again. He shouted
back. Listened. An answering shout. They must have come up
the river in search of him. The shouting came again; the river
must be over there. He moved cautiously, calling, listening for
the response, making his way in their direction. The sounds
were louder now, waking the jungle night. Then he heard them,
the snapping of branches as they forced their way towards him.
And suddenly they were there. John Cross, Brian and two of the
guerrillas, bursting through the dense undergrowth, half-
dragging, half-carrying him to the river, into the sampan, back
to camp.

On their return they immediately put him to bed and within
a short time he was delirious, his teeth chattering and his
emaciated body shaking in uncontrollable spasms so that the
whole bed rattled. By the time they switched on the evening
news bulletin he was quieter and the fever appeared to have
broken.

When the bulletin was over, he sat up, rolled a cigarette and
said, 'Never mind, the news is good!' The others could not have
been more amazed if the dead had spoken.

The news was indeed good. In Europe the Allied forces were
still racing across France in pursuit of the fleeing Germans.
Most of Belgium had been liberated and the vital port of
Ostend captured. The Russians were still outside Warsaw but
in the south were pouring into Bulgaria. The Americans were
poised for the invasion of the Philippines and in North Burma
the enemy licked their wounds as they waited for the inevitable
advance of the 14th Army.

Meanwhile the Japanese were mounting an all-out operation
to eliminate the guerrillas in South Johore. By the end of
September they were engaging Communist units in every area.
They came to Tengkil in force, bringing planks and *atap* thatch
to build a permanent barracks. However, within a few days the
guerrillas had managed to set fire to the materials and destroy
them.

The radio situation was serious. The charging engine had
broken down finally and, although Cross and his men had
acquired a motor-cycle engine from Tengkil, they were now
unable to get anyone back there to pick up the parts which were

necessary to adapt the engine so that it would charge the batteries. Within a month the last battery was dead.

Japanese patrols left Tengkil every day and scoured the countryside, returning to their base in the village each night. Their stranglehold on the district was not only affecting the repair of the charging engine; food was scarce and what little there was thoroughly unpalatable. The British missed the heartening boost to their spirits which the evening news had given them and now they had nothing to alleviate the depressing effect of their miserable jungle camp. Furthermore, in addition to frequent bouts of malaria they now had diarrhoea as well, which left them with feelings of nausea for their meagre rations.

The situation could not be allowed to continue, especially as the guerrillas were also becoming affected by illness. John Cross tackled 'Charlie', pointing out that the camp was unhealthy and that most of them were sick. They had no radio news with which to produce the newspaper and the food was ghastly. In his view, they were serving no useful purpose here and he urged a move to a better camp out of the jungle.

'Charlie' dug in his heels, saying that they could not move until the Japanese had left Tengkil. But Cross saw that he was really reluctant to move without the sanction of 4th Guerrilla HQ. He replied angrily that if HQ could not do better than they were doing, it was time to take matters into their own hands. This altercation caused a temporary rift between the two men and for several days they did not speak to each other. However, a reconciliation was at last made and 'Charlie' promised to take the matter up with HQ on his next visit.

What actually happened on his next visit was that 'Charlie' was posted elsewhere and a replacement was sent, named Ah Gang, with whom Cross found it impossible to work. Ah Gang owed his position purely to his academic and political achievements and was in no way suited to organizing the practical side of life in the jungle. Cross wanted to move down-river to a camp run by Ta Ching, with whom he had had satisfactory dealings in the past, and he and Ah Gang went to see him. But Ta Ching would not discuss anything in the presence of Ah Gang and refused to have the radio party in his camp without permission from HQ.

Ah Gang refused to take Cross to see Ah Ti at HQ but agreed

to go himself, taking with him a letter from Cross. For five days Cross waited for his return, the delay only helping to confirm his belief that Ta Ching's camp was a far better site than theirs. His anxiety increased over the rest of his party, sitting in their gloomy jungle camp, sick and on the verge of starvation.

At last Ah Gang came back with a letter from Ah Ti in which he agreed to the move. It had taken six weeks to get the transfer authorized, and it was plain from the difficulty with which they made the journey that permission had come not a moment too soon.

While these frustrating negotiations were going on, 'Waggy' decided to try, with Jim's assistance, to repair the big end of the connecting rod of the charging engine. His method was a masterpeice of improvization. The casing of the motor-cycle gearbox was made of a soft metal which he could melt. He made a wooden mould, in two halves, packed each half with stiff clay and made an impression in the clay with the broken big end. He then poured molten metal into the mould and allowed it to cool. Jim then spent several hours with a hacksaw and file helping 'Waggy' to shape the new big end, which they finally fitted into the engine. It ran for five hours before breaking down again, but by that time one battery had been charged and they were able to go on the air.

They set to and manufactured another during the next few days and this one was more successful, lasting for over fifteen hours, enough to recharge all the batteries. It was a triumph of ingenuity, the work had helped to pass the time and it meant that they were once more in touch with the outside world. There the news was partly good, partly bad. The Allied advance across Europe had been brought to a halt after the failure at Arnhem, but the Japanese fleet had been trounced at Leyte Gulf and the Americans were ashore in the Philippines.

Meanwhile the Sakai returned. When they left they had intended to join another tribe related to them, but it had moved and they had been unable to find it. After friendly assurances had been given to them by the guerrillas, they set up camp nearby, which pleased everyone.

When he had finished working on the engine, Jim decided to try and get some fish from the river. The water was rather shallow near the camp and he had limited success, but at least it was something to do. One day he was slashing with his *parang* at bushes on the river bank so as to get a better position from which to fish, when he suddenly saw, right under his nose, an enormous snake coiled up in the bush he was cutting. Arresting his *parang* in mid-swing just in time, he leapt back and ran to look for a Chinese called 'Lefty' who was known to be an authority on snakes. This man had no fingers on his right hand as a result of an accident in a saw-mill, hence his name; nevertheless he killed the snake with a single blow from his heavy stick. It was a coloured python and the guerrillas said it would make good eating. Duly cooked, everyone including Jim agreed that it was excellent.

Although Jim still had bad bouts of fever they did not leave him feeling as weak in the legs as before. He knew that the others always worried about him when he was ill but he himself was not particularly concerned now that he was back in their care. It seemed to him that this was one of the best camps he had ever been in. The Sakai had cleared about three and a half acres and there were ample gardens in which they grew sweet potatoes and tobacco, more than enough to provide them with food and enabling them to celebrate Christmas, 1944, in some style. But the greatest joy was to be out in the open again, to see the sky and feel the sun on his skin.

In a deeper part of the river Jim took up his swimming lessons again and eventually managed to swim for quite a distance. He also had better luck fishing from a sampan which he anchored near a bank under overhanging branches which concealed him and yet allowed him to see up and down the river. He had been in the bush for so long now, and he spent so much time out on his own, that, subconsciously, he had acquired some of the wariness of the wild jungle creatures. The Sakai had taught him how to make fish traps by blocking the river with stakes so that the fish had to pass through a narrow channel, and he caught several in this way. Once he trapped a gigantic bull-frog, nearly four feet long when hung up by the legs. It was delicious to eat, but it was the only one he ever saw.

All the British occupied one hut, away from the river and on the edge of the jungle, which they shared with the two Chinese radio operators from Barry's party. One, Liu Chin Hung, slept next to Jim and as he spoke broken English they were able to have long talks together. He was a follower of Chiang Kai-shek and did not like the Communists much. Cheong Khuen, the engine fitter, also visited them, and he made Jim his own personal *parang*.

At night they took turns at guard duty. One night when Jim was on guard near the cookhouse he heard someone, or some animal, moving in the darkness. He kept dead still and the noise stopped. Quietly he crept back to the hut and roused one of the Chinese. Together in the faint moonlight they saw an animal as big as a sheep, striped like a zebra, eating the potato tops. The guerrilla sprang forward and killed it with a stick. Jim never found out what animal it was but it provided them with several good meals. (In retrospect he thinks it must have been a wild goat *(kambing gurun)* which is rare and normally lives on mountain tops. The 'stripes' could have been light and shade in the moonlight. He did not see it in daylight as it was cut up and cooked that night, but he remembers that it had a hairy coat.)

The New Year brought positive evidence of the changing fortunes of the war in the East, a formation of B29s roaring past on their way to Singapore, the sunlight glinting on their wings. The sound was quite different from that made by the occasional Japanese aircraft, and Jim remembered hearing it a couple of months earlier, but he had been unable to identify it then.

Before long the planes returned, pursued by darting Japanese fighters which seemed to have no effect at all on the huge bombers as they swept swiftly north. 'Waggy' had switched on the radio and they were able to listen to the American crews talking to each other. Jim heard one pilot say to another, 'Why didn't you fire at that kite behind me?'

It was an exhilarating moment. Jim felt tears in his eyes, and his legs were trembling: so near, but still so far. Yet hope, so often almost extinguished, bubbled up once more, and with nearly unendurable tension.

Events began to move fast. The next day Cross received two letters from Captain Davis, whom he had been trying to contact for nearly two years. Davis said that he was not at present in touch with the Allies and he sent Cross a coded message to send out if he was able to do so. Cross was not in touch with the Allies either so he was unable to transmit this signal. Davis also added a cryptic reference to 'friends' who should by now have met up with Cross. Could this mean that Allied forces had been dropped in Johore by parachute during one of the B29 raids? If so, it was an exciting development. Cross replied to the letters, asking for more details of the 'friends'.

Meanwhile they could do little except go on with their day-to-day life in the camp, swimming and growing vegetables and tobacco, but they felt increasingly restless and eager to do more. However, there was plenty of action elsewhere. General Rundstedt's desperate counter-attack in the Ardennes had finally been held and this was to prove the last effective operation by German armour. The Japanese were reeling back as General Slim opened his final offensive to drive them out of Burma, and Royal Naval aircraft had struck at the oilfields at Palembang in south Sumatra.

The information they were waiting for came at the end of January. A letter, signed by Ah Ti but written in better English than he would have been capable of, was quite casually handed to Cross just as they were sitting down to their afternoon meal. It said that a British party, commanded by a Major W. B. Martin, who carried credentials from Lord Louis Mountbatten, had arrived in Johore. It added that Major Martin knew about Cross and his party and would visit them in February.

This was really dramatic news. However, there was no sense in changing the pattern of their existence and so they continued with their gardening routine, sharing the work of their Chinese comrades with whom relations had never been better. There was one exception – Ah Gui, the armourer/blacksmith. He was very anti-European and a fanatical Communist. His small knowledge of mechanical contrivances had given him a peculiar authority among the guerrillas and he began to use this advantage to upset 'Waggy'. First he took some of their valuable stock of petrol; then he demanded that the last pieces of the white-metal casing of the motor-cycle gear box should be given to him for making bombs. Cross would not agree to this and he wrote to the local directing party and to Ah Ti at 4th HQ, stating the case and asking whether Ah Gui's demands were to be met or not. The answer was a clear-cut 'no' and this did nothing to lessen the hostility which the Chinese armourer felt towards the British.

February passed without any further communication from Major Martin. Then, in early March, came bad news. The group in Johore had received an air supply drop one moonlight night. The Japanese had either seen it, or had been told about it, and a force of about a hundred of them had moved in under cover of darkness. At dawn they charged the hut where the party was living, killing Martin and some of the Chinese. The others fled into the jungle and escaped, although for several days they were split up and hunted by the Japanese. By a stroke of luck Martin's Chinese radio operator had not been in the camp and had the radio with him, so contact with India was not lost. He wrote at once asking for details of Cross's party and Cross replied immediately. Within the next fortnight the survivors of Martin's party managed to re-group and on 20 March Cross received a letter asking him to come south and meet them.

He set off next day accompanied by 'Waggy', Lee Boon as interpreter, and Ta Yu. It was good to be travelling light, instead of humping heavy radio equipment as they normally did, and it was stimulating to be going through new territory. They started their journey in the usual way, being poled down the river in a sampan by the Sakai, but they came ashore well upstream of the old staging post because, since the killing of 'Peg Leg', this had been continually watched by the Japanese.

They took a well-concealed route and at regular intervals they changed guides. This was a safety precaution: no one guide knew the entire route which lessened the risk of its betrayal. At the first stop they had a meal and dropped Ta Yu, continuing with a new guide. They spent that night on the site of the old HQ camp, most of which had been burned down by the Japanese, only a few derelict huts still standing. Early in the morning they crossed Tengkil sands; the guide, who was familiar with the regular habits of Japanese patrols, knowing they were safe there at that hour. All the same, they were glad when they were across that bare and exposed expanse and back in cover.

Exhausted by their journey, they staggered into the 4th Independent Party's new HQ at dusk and went early to bed as they were told that the next day's march would be a hard one. It was indeed, and the pace set by the guide was so fast that neither of the two soldiers had breath left to talk to each other. Late in the afternoon they came out of the jungle and crossed cultivated land until at last they arrived at a Malay *kampong* on the bank of a river. Here they washed, had their best meal for two years and smoked factory-made cheroots and cigarettes before turning in.

They had just finished an excellent breakfast when Ah Ti arrived to have a conference with them. Cross noticed that he put particular emphasis on the fact that the guerrillas were now AJF (Anti-Japanese Forces) working in conjunction with Allied Forces, and no longer MCP (Malayan Communist Party).

Later that morning, Major Sime, who had taken over command of Major Martin's party, strode out of the jungle accompanied by one of their old guerrilla friends, nicknamed 'Little Elephant', who was now well-dressed in British uniform and carried a Tommy gun. Sime was hardly able to conceal his surprise at finding that Cross and 'Waggy' were not physical wrecks after their years in the jungle. He explained that his party was concerned only with operations against the Japanese, and that as Cross's party really came under the heading of 'Intelligence' he would send a signal to India recommending that they should be taken to an Intelligence party near the east coast. This group, commanded by a Major J. V. Hart, had been landed by submarine late in 1944 but life in the jungle had undermined the health of some of its members and they were to be evacuated, also by submarine. Sime thought that Cross's party, including Jim and Brian, might be taken off at the same time, so he told them to return to camp, pack up everything ready to hand over to the guerrillas and await orders to move. Bidding them farewell and good luck, he disappeared into the jungle to return to his base.

Cross and 'Waggy' remained in the *kampong* for the rest of the day. Ah Ti came to see them again and, although they talked on many subjects, his main theme was that the new arrivals neither understood nor completely trusted the guerrillas. He urged Cross to persuade them to give arms to the Chinese so that they could fight alongside the British. Cross asked him point-blank what he would do with weapons once the war was over. Ah Ti parried the question by saying that they should concern themselves now with defeating the Japanese and not worry about what might happen afterwards.

The next morning they embarked in a *sampan*. The craft was so heavily loaded that they only had a few inches of freeboard.

Fruit trees overhung the river and they managed to shoot two monkeys out of them for their evening meal. Before they landed, at midday, they were almost swamped by torrential rain and could only keep afloat by baling continuously. All afternoon they sloshed through the sodden undergrowth, soaked to the skin, until they came to a small hut where they managed to light a fire and cooked the monkey which they ate with black beans and rice. Afterwards they sat crammed together in the hut, smoking and talking, and for once Ah Ti kept off politics.

They had hoped that by using the *sampan* they would cut a day off their journey, but the next morning the heavy rains had so swollen the river that they had great difficulty in making any headway against the fast-running current. As the floods were well over the banks they were able to cut across the normal loops of the river, two paddling and two pulling themselves forward by bushes. Their soaking clothes impeded them so they stripped off, only to find that leeches then crawled unhindered all over their bodies, necessitating frequent pauses to remove them.

By late afternoon they were all exhausted, even Ta Yu, and as they were only half-way back to the camp he decided to stop and take them to an old shack in the jungle. He knew that hidden there were a cooking pot, rice and matches, for the use of couriers who might become benighted. They pulled the boat out of the water and set off, but it was dark before they reached the hut. Here they spent a miserable night.

They finally reached the Sakai camp the following afternoon, with plenty to tell the others about their trip and about the possibility of being evacuated by submarine. Amid the general excitement, Jim was very quiet.

'I don't suppose they'll bother with chaps like us, will they?' he asked, meaning himself and Brian.

'Of course they bloody well will!' retorted Cross almost angrily. Poor old Jim! So tough, yet so humble. He couldn't believe that Authority would be bothered with him or make any effort to pull him out.

Soon after the return of Cross and 'Waggy' a message came that they were to move on 1 April, which was only a few days away. They packed up all their apparatus ready to hand over to the guerrillas, and a farewell party was given for them. The highlight of the feast was a *rusu*, a deer about the size of a red deer, which one of the Sakai had killed while it was swimming down the river.

Jim spent these last few days in a state of mental turmoil. Excitement, incredulity, apprehension at the prospect of resuming 'normal' life, kept him in a state of nervous tension that was almost unbearable. But the others were so jubilant that gradually he too began to accept the fact that he really might be going home.

When the time came to say goodbye, Cheong Khuen was so downcast that Jim, on an impulse, gave him his precious cigarette case. In return Cheong Khuen gave Jim a 50 yuan Chunking banknote, the only valuable he possessed. Jim still has it. Lee Boon and Liu Chin Hung were staying behind and, as he said goodbye, the latter lost his usual Chinese impassivity and was openly weeping.

Lee Boon had organized his Sakai girls' singing class to 'sing them out' and, as the *sampan* left the landing stage, the choir, drawn up on the bank at the first bend of the river, broke out into 'Will ye no come back again?' and then changed to 'Auld Lang Syne'. All recognized that these were remarkable additions to their normal repertoire of political songs.

It was a moment charged with emotion and Jim found that tears were pouring down his cheeks. He was leaving his Chinese companions who had been such good friends to him and the jungle, which had so often nearly destroyed him, now seemed to be enticing him to stay.

CHAPTER THIRTEEN

Journey Towards Freedom

For two hours the Sakai poled them down the river, passing the old camp to which Jim and Brian had returned after Barry's expedition. Soon after this their guide, a man they did not know, who spoke so little Malay that communication with him was difficult, directed them to pull in to the east bank. Here they clambered ashore and entered the jungle.

Sime had told them to travel light and, apart from a few personal possessions, each carried only a small bag of rice, while the guide carried the cooking pot. They marched for five hours and then made camp on a mountainside where there was a waterfall and a cave in which they could shelter. Before they had finished cooking their meal a heavy rainstorm struck them and soon the waterfall became a deafening torrent which drowned all conversation. Water seeped in through the earth roof of the cave, flooding the floor so that they had to cut poles and lay them on rocks in order to keep themselves dry.

Within an hour Jim had become delirious with a severe attack of fever. He lay shaking and moaning, 'I'm cold, Cross, I'm cold.' All they could do was pile their blankets on him. By the time the rain had stopped he had at last fallen into a deep sleep. Gently they peeled the wet blankets off him and wrapped him in the only one which they had managed to keep dry. Then they wrung the water out of the others and tried, without much success, to get some sleep themselves.

Having a sick man on their hands at this point really gummed up the works, Cross thought. The guide would probably insist on carrying out his orders to complete the journey over his part of the route, sending someone back to the cave to look after Jim until he was fit to go on. But then how would he ever catch them up? They could not stay with him and send the guide on ahead with the bad news because they did not know where they were, or where they were heading, or the way back to the Sakai camp. And how were they going to discuss any action with this unfamiliar guide who spoke so little Malay?

After a miserable night of snatched sleep they woke, limbs stiff and chilled to the marrow of their bones. In the first light of dawn they looked with concern at Jim. He was awake, hollow-eyed and deathly pale.

'How are you feeling, Jim?' Cross asked him. With a wan smile he answered, 'I'm not missing that bloody submarine, if that's what you're thinking.'

'Good lad,' said Cross. 'We'll see you don't.'

Jim felt desperately weak as he struggled to his feet. He wondered if he would be able to reach the next camp. Gone was the fleeting nostalgia he had felt only yesterday for this impossible land, which had harboured him, and so often nearly killed him, and had almost become home, of a sort. He was damned if it was going to get him as it had got the others.

Soon after leaving camp they came out into cultivated country where the warmth of the sun drew the stiffness out of their aching bones. Even Jim revived a little as he staggered along, determined to keep up with the others. He knew this path as he had often used it when he had been at the old HQ camp. During the morning they passed the burnt-out compound and he saw a pile of ashes which was all that was left of the hut where he, Brian, Douglas and Fred had spent eight months together. After a rest they pushed on, crossing the swamp where the path lay over floating poles, and came to the old guerrilla hospital which had also been burnt to the ground.

Here they stopped for the night and, while they cut down some big leaves to lie on, being too tired to bother with making a shelter, the guide cooked rice and gave them each a tin of Fussell's evaporated milk which had recently been parachuted to the guerrillas.

The following day they came to Tengkil sands, where they saw no sign of any civilians, and where the sawmill and all the huts had been reduced to ashes. As the Japanese were still in the village in considerable force they had to make a wide detour.

Eventually they camped on a hill in the jungle where there were some old deserted huts and a number of graves. All night long it poured with rain and they were constantly getting up to patch their dilapidated roof.

At dawn next day they went on through the jungle. At one point they heard voices and presently came upon a sawmill where many men were at work. There did not seem to be any Japanese there, but they gave it a wide berth anyway, as it was important that they should not be seen even by friendly natives. Throughout the day rain fell relentlessly and they were all thoroughly wet and tired when at last they came to a guerrilla camp. 'Charlie' was waiting there to greet them and his first words were, 'I think you are all going home to England.' To the weary Cross, this bald statement seemed totally unreal.

At it turned out, they had to wait in that camp for ten days, a maddening delay, but unavoidable as heavy rain had made the next stage of their route impassable. Also, it seemed, the party was to be augmented by three American airmen who had been shot down and who were now to be evacuated with them in the submarine.

At last the floods subsided, but there was no sign of the three airmen. Nevertheless, 'Charlie' decided that they should push on, leaving a guide to bring the Americans later. Not far from the camp they had to make a hazardous crossing of the still-swollen river, and they were nearly swept off the bridge poles as they clung to the *rattan* hand-line. No sooner had they reached the other side than they saw the missing airmen splashing through the flood water towards them, and they were able to continue the journey together.

The Americans, it seemed, had baled out when their B29 had been hit during a raid on Singapore in January. Of the original five who got out, two were captured, taken to Singapore, paraded naked round the city and then publicly beheaded. The other three, one of them wounded, landed separately but were picked up and spirited away by guerrillas and, like other servicemen in occupied Malaya, had been taken care of by them. After three months in one of the guerrilla camps, they were brought to join Cross's party. The Americans had not taken to jungle life and had found three months of it more than enough. When one of them casually asked Cross how long the British had been there and was told, 'Three and a quarter years,' he exclaimed, 'Jesus Christ!' and lapsed into a stunned silence.

Jim asked the Chinese guide how much further they had to go that day, but he only got the usual reply, '*Ti dapa*' (It doesn't matter). It was in fact a five-hour march and they camped for the night just south of Bukit Muntahak. Here 'Waggy' went down with fever. He rolled himself up in several blankets and tried to sweat it out, as they were now coming to the most dangerous part of the journey which involved a crossing of the Kota Tinggi–Singapore road. The camp was also occupied by a small guerrilla fighting patrol, who reported that they had been in contact with Japanese forces almost daily during the previous week. This news brought home to Cross's party once again the many hazards which still lay between them and that submarine.

In the morning they waited, resting, while the Chinese reconnoitred the way ahead. Finding it all clear, the party moved on, arriving in the vicinity of the road at dusk. During the march they skirted a timber yard and came out on to a cart track which ran from a rubber estate to the main road. Here they waited while the Chinese sent scouts ahead to check the route again.

When it was quite dark one of the scouts came back and whispered to the guide, who led them forward and presently gave a low call which was answered by a scout at the roadside. They closed up into a tight bunch and received their final instructions in whispers. To get on to the track which led away east towards Hart's camp they would have to travel for some distance south in single file on the edge of the road. No one was to utter a sound and contact was to be maintained by keeping a hand on the man immediately in front. In the event of an alarm they were to dash individually into cover and try to regroup later.

Walking on the road was a pleasant change from creeping through the jungle and the pace became faster and faster until those at the back of the party had to trot in order to keep up with the leaders. Suddenly the men in front of Cross dashed into the bushes on the left; Cross followed the scramble and fell into a deep gully. No sooner had he regained his feet than Jim crashed in head-first on top of him, knocking him flat again. They crouched breathless and tense as the headlights of a lorry came round a bend and swept the road which they had left only seconds earlier.

They waited silently, wondering if the Japanese had spotted them. As it climbed the slope the lorry changed gear several times so that it seemed as if it was about to stop. The British and Chinese were unarmed except for a few revolvers and one hand-grenade which the guide carried attached to his belt. In the light of the headlamps they could see him fumbling with this, as if he intended to throw it at the lorry and its occupants. Mercifully he changed his mind; the lorry ground slowly past, and when the sound of its engine had finally died away they scrambled out of cover and back on to the road.

They came at last to a cart track running off to the east and plunged eagerly down it. But before long they heard voices ahead of them and, as there was no handy gully in which to hide, they leapt up the bank into some thick bushes. Unfortunately the bushes concealed a barbed wire fence, and all they could do was hang motionless from it until the voices, which turned out to be those of Chinese civilians, had passed and died away.

Continuing down the track, they arrived at the village where they were supposed to spend the night. But the guerrillas who were waiting there for them made them go on into the jungle before they stopped. They suspected that someone had informed on them because a Chinese who had been sent ahead the previous day to buy coffee and supplies – incidentally with the party's last 250 dollars – had been picked up by the Japanese as soon as he reached Kota Tinggi.

It was three in the morning before they halted, too tired even to make any sort of bed. Cross settled himself in the fork of a tree and the others made themselves as comfortable as they could. During the march Jim and Brian had been ragging the guerrillas for getting in such a panic every time they heard even Chinese voices approaching, and had suggested that they should hand over their arms to the British soldiers who would not be so nervous. As they dozed Jim heard his old friend 'Janker Wallah' taking the guerrillas to task for their timidity.

During the night they were joined by other guerrillas who had caught the traitor of Kota Tinggi and brought him along with them. As usual he was trussed from neck to wrists which were tied behind his back, but he seemed remarkably cheerful considering that he must have known he would be executed.

They went on at daybreak and struggled for several hours through mangrove swamps, walking on the roots with water up to their waists. At midday they reached dry land and entered a guerrilla camp where they burned the leeches off themselves, had a wash and a meal and were soon asleep. Cross found that he knew many of the guerrillas here as they had helped his party to enter the jungle, not far from this spot, over three years earlier. Their leader, whom he had also met before, said that the traitor would be beheaded in the morning and offered Cross the privilege of doing this, which he declined.

Next day they marched for about five hours and came to a dry part of the jungle where the ground was covered in dead leaves. These obliterated their footprints when at last they left the track and followed the final approach to Major Hart's camp. The first leg of their journey to freedom had taken them seventeen days.

Major Hart's party, code-name 'Mint', consisted of a Captain, a Lieutenant (Douglas Browning, an ex-planter) and a Sergeant. They were all members of Force 136. This organization sent parties of specially trained men into occupied South-East Asia to supply the guerrillas with arms and collect information. They were operating in Johore from 1944 onwards and were either dropped by parachute or landed by submarine. Among them were a number of Chinese agents whose job was to gather intelligence which Hart then transmitted by radio to his HQ in India.

This was both novel and exhilarating for the jungle survivors; for Major Hart and his men were not simply the woebegone remnant of a defeated army, left behind after a retreat; they were the symbol of promised victory. They had come into the country from the outside, with which they were in regular contact, fitted out with light, modern weapons, proper clothing, medicines and so forth. All these factors roused in Jim and the others feelings both of expectancy and reassurance: they were no longer 'missing, presumed dead': they might still be missing, technically speaking, indeed to their families they were; but suddenly their daily fear of lonely obliteration receded, and for the first time in years they felt a tangible hope of escape, of a safe return.

Cross went down with malaria almost as soon as they arrived, but the others got to work on a small shack which they enlarged so that it would hold all of them, including the three Americans, on one long sleeping platform. The Force 136 men had light and sophisticated equipment, including mosquito nets and hammocks, but Jim thought that he and his comrades were better off living in the simple way that they had known for so long, as this left them with little to carry on the march. On the other hand, he saw that great strides had been made in the design of weapons and equipment suitable for fighting in jungle. Light semi-automatic American carbines and Sten guns were a tremendous improvement on the old rifles and Tommy guns. Jungle-green uniform was much less conspicuous than the khaki drill in which he had had to fight, and they now had canvas and rubber boots which laced up to the knee. Not only were these more silent, more waterpoof and lighter than the old heavily-studded leather boots but they even kept out the leeches to some extent.

The food in this camp, however, consisted only of potatoes and local vegetables, and while the survivors were quite used to it, the others found it thin fare. But an aerial drop of supplies was due at the next full moon and this held promise of better things.

Hart, a solitary man by nature, lived in a tiny hut away from the main camp and he called them up there one at a time to tell their stories and to give him any information they could which would add to his collection of Intelligence material. Cross spent a long evening talking to Hart and answering his questions. He found him a good listener, who did not interrupt or argue with any opinions he expressed.

During their conversation Cross also learned more about Hart himself. Born of Dutch and English parents, he had been educated in England and had gone on to qualify in forestry. He had taken up planting in Java and loved the country and its people so much that he intended to live out his life there. His career in forestry had made him both independent and self-sufficient, so he was a good choice for this clandestine work, but he had hoped to be sent on a mission to Java and considered Malaya very much second-best. He was still under thirty years old, well over six feet tall, and his somewhat languid manner concealed great vitality and endurance, as they were to see later during their arduous march to the coast.

Hart asked Jim and Brian to come and see him together. He heard them out and was obviously impressed that they had managed to survive so many hardships for so long. Indeed, he promised to put in a report on their courage and tenacity when he returned to India. He told them about the submarine which would, he said, be bringing in supplies and arms, and also about the air drop. 'I'm glad to have you here,' he said. 'We're short-handed, and we can do with help, both around the camp and also to recover that drop.'

He fitted them out with green uniforms and jungle boots and gave them a choice of weapons. Brian Smith selected a carbine and Jim a Sten gun with four spare loaded magazines, light and a joy to handle. Then he told them that, if everything went according to plan, he would like them to get away in the submarine. After a moment's thought the two soldiers looked at each other, and then with one accord asked him if he wanted them to stay, as Lieutenant Browning was also due to leave and that would reduce Hart's party to two British and himself.

Hart studied them for a moment in silence as he weighed up their offer. Then, with a warm smile, he said, 'No. You've earned your trip home.' He added drily, 'Besides, we're not there yet.'

Relief, and a twinge of disappointment, followed his refusal; having survived so far, it would have been good to see the Japanese finally disposed of. If Douglas and Fred were still alive, it might have been another matter; yet the truth was that none of them would have been fit enough for active service. Jim and Brian certainly were not.

A day or two later they went with Hart to select a suitable site for the impending supply drop. On the way back Brian shot a leopard and they brought some of the meat back to camp. But alas, it was quite inedible – just tough, stringy muscle which no amount of cooking could improve.

The Japanese undoubtedly knew that Allied forces were operating in Johore, and their aircraft scoured the jungle at tree-top height looking for signs of activity. One afternoon Jim and almost everyone else in the camp were posing for a group photograph when an enemy plane skimmed the trees directly overhead, but the pilot presumably saw nothing as it did not return.

At last the date for the supply drop arrived, amid mounting excitement. At midday everyone went out to the dropping zone, a long strip of open ground covered with *resam* (bracken). They set up their recognition signal, a large 'T' marked out by sticks, with a piece of inflammable rubber on the top of each stick. By nightfall they had made all their preparations and settled down silently to wait, straining their ears for the sound of an aircraft engine. After what seemed like an age, they heard a distant drone, and as it gradually grew louder they all prayed fervently that it was not Japanese. Only Hart remained ice-calm, staring into the sky with his night glasses and listening intently.

The drone grew to a roar as a huge Liberator came into view overhead. Hart flashed the recognition sign with his signal lamp and simultaneously each man standing by the sticks which formed the 'T' lit the pieces of rubber attached to them. The aircraft banked and turned and roared in again over the tree-tops, loosing a cascade of parachutes which opened out and gently wafted the canisters to the ground. Then, flashing a farewell signal on its navigation lights, the Liberator sped away north on its journey back to India.

They stood in total silence until the sound of the plane had died away, listening for any evidence of Japanese aircraft. Satisfied that there was none, they quickly set about collecting the stores. The memory of what had happened to Major Martin's party, which had been caught in the dropping zone, was sharp in their minds. They buried the parachutes which had reached the ground; those which had become entangled high up in the trees they had to leave for the time being; all they could do was to cut loose the canisters and hope that the Japanese would not spot the parachutes from the air before they could be cleared away. Then they hurried back to camp, carrying as much as they could, having hidden the rest of the stores in a dump for future collection. The drop had included good food, drink and cigarettes; and even Jim, who had been fighting an attack of malaria throughout the night's work, soon felt well enough to enjoy them with the others.

Next day they made the first of several trips to bring in the dumped stores and retrieve the tangled parachutes. On one of these expeditions a pig ran across the track and Brian killed it with his first shot. It turned out to be a domestic sow from a nearby *kampong* and the infuriated owner was not long in coming to the camp and demanding recompense. He threatened to report them to the Japanese if they would not pay him for his loss. The price of pork was very high on the Singapore market, and he said the sow's nine piglets would probably die too, so he claimed a total of £350. Cross paid him with Japanese military currency – which he thought would soon be worthless anyway – but Brian came in for a good deal of ribbing from the others who told him that it would be stopped out of his pay after the war. Brian took it seriously until they realized this and put him out of his misery. Carriers were sent out to collect the sow, which was vast, and they all gorged themselves on pork.

At about this time news came through that Germany had surrendered and the war in Europe was over. The party was in high spirits, knowing that now the full weight of Allied power could be directed solely against the Japanese. Already Rangoon had been captured by a sea-borne invasion without opposition, the Japanese garrison having withdrawn towards Siam. The survivors of the ill-fated 'March on Delhi' were being driven south, hammered continually by the 14th Army. Burmese guerrillas and local hill tribes had risen against them, and starving stragglers were ambushed as they left the Pegu Yomas to cross the open plains of South Burma in a last desperate effort to reach the Sittang River. Skeletons dressed in tatters, suffering from cholera, malaria and starvation, and with every man's hand against them, many found that they could go no further and lay down to die. Those who did reach the Sittang were killed in their thousands before they could cross. Many must have remembered with bitterness those days, only three years earlier, when it had been the Japanese who were marching to victory and who had so nearly destroyed the retreating Allied forces at this same bridge. Their operations in Burma were to cost the Japanese one hundred and ninety thousand dead, and this figure did not include the undiscovered bodies of those who had died during their retreat through the jungle.

Jim felt a grim satisfaction that these soldiers who had so mercilessly murdered and raped their way through South-East Asia in the days of their triumph were at last paying the price for their bestial conduct. Remembering the massacres of his comrades and the many atrocities committed against helpless Chinese civilians, he could feel no shred of pity for the Japanese now.

One of the agents whom Major Hart had sent to Singapore to gather information now returned to the camp. He was a brilliant and audacious Chinese who had obtained work with the Japanese and was allowed in and out of the naval base and docks. Jim asked him about the Allied POWs there, and was told that both they and the Chinese were still being ill-treated. The agent described a shocking scene he had himself witnessed, when the Japanese had taken a Chinese dock worker, put his head in a big vice, and at intervals tightened it until the man's skull cracked like a nut.

On his way back through Johore the agent had seen many POWs making tunnels for ambushes, digging slit-trenches and building huge earth walls round dumps of supplies. This could only mean that the Japanese were expecting an Allied invasion. But they had also announced that they were proposing to put POWs into the front line when the Allies attacked, and that any not killed then they would themselves kill. Typical, Jim thought to himself.

The Japanese rightly suspected that the increased aerial activity over Johore was the prelude to an invasion of Malaya, and they stepped up their search operations, even bringing in forces from other parts of South-East Asia. Their concentrations of troops near the roads and in the rubber plantations made life difficult and hazardous for the guerrilla forces, and Hart was anxious that the submarine party should get away before the Japanese started to harry him.

When the signal about their future arrived in May, it said that at least one member of the radio party should come to India to be interrogated in detail, and that the others could choose either to come out or to remain with Force 136. Cross discussed this with Morter and 'Waggy'. All three of them would have liked to see the thing through; but at the same time Cross knew that their military knowledge was now three years out of date. Best, perhaps, to go out, catch up with developments, and then come back. To this Morter and 'Waggy' agreed: they would stick together.

Before long they received orders to leave on 27 May for a beach between Tanjong Lompat and Tanjong Siang. They now had a date for departure and a place to go to, but they were not prepared yet to believe it would ever happen.

During their farewell party they all signed a Japanese-occupation ten dollar note. On the reverse side someone wrote the ribald comment, 'Before we had these we used to use leaves.'

CHAPTER FOURTEEN

The Rendezvous

The journey started easily enough; the jungle was sparse and the ground level. But this terrain soon gave way to swamps and for eight hours they waded through muddy water, sometimes up to their necks. Hart, six foot six inches tall, led them on indefatigably, but Jim often had to hold his Sten gun above his head when the water reached his chin.

When at last they arrived at their next camp, a dry spot in a coconut grove, several of them were obviously not fit to go on and Hart said they could have a day's rest. Here Jim drank coconut milk for the first time and found it delicious. There was a large well-built house on the site, occupied by a somewhat eccentric middle-aged Chinese couple. Jim was always astonished when he came to a place like this, as he had often done, and found a good house with people living in it, surrounded by miles of uninhabited swamp or jungle.

He and Brian had not been unduly exhausted by the first day's march, so the following morning they set off again with some of the guerrillas, leaving the rest of the party to come on when they had recovered. They marched for three and a half hours, partly through swamps, though nothing like as deep as those of the previous day, and came to a small river which they crossed. From here they could smell the sea, and before long they came to a beach. They made a rough camp about a hundred yards inland, just cutting big leaves to lie on as they could not be bothered to build a shelter.

The sea! Suddenly the possibility that he really might be about to leave the jungle, that he might actually return home to Norfolk, became tantalizingly real to Jim. At the same time he felt a stab of pain, remembering all those – Tom Showell, Fred, Douglas and the rest – whom the jungle had claimed. It tinged his anticipation with a profound sadness.

That evening some more guerrillas arrived at the camp, several of whom Jim knew. In the morning, careful to keep under cover, they all went down to the beach and had a good look at it. They could see why this particular spot had been chosen for the pick-up. On either side of the bay, sheltering it from inquisitive eyes, were mangrove swamps, while the beach itself was smooth sand.

During the afternoon the rest of the party turned up. Next morning they hoisted a large yellow oblong flag in the vertical position, where it could be seen from the sea. This was a pre-arranged signal to the submarine meaning 'All clear, come in tonight'. If anything occurred ashore which might threaten the evacuation, the flag was to be turned to the horizontal position, which meant 'Keep off. Try again tomorrow night'. The Royal Navy, although very skilled in these clandestine operations, was always understandably reluctant to hazard a submarine and its highly-trained crew in shallow inshore waters just to pick up or land small parties of soldiers or agents. It was the understood thing that, if there was any doubt at all about the safety of the operation, naval considerations would take priority over the needs of the army.

Hardly had they put up the recognition signal than there was an alarm. A fishing boat came in and grounded on the beach and three Malays sprang ashore. As soon as they were close enough the watchers in the undergrowth charged out and seized them. The three men protested that they were only going to visit some relatives who lived inland, but no one was inclined to take any chances. They pulled the boat up the beach, concealed it and locked the men in a nearby hut with some food. The windows were shuttered and the Malays were told that no harm would befall them if they kept quiet, and that they would be released the following morning. They seemed to be quite innocent and even friendly but everyone felt uneasy in case they were collaborators sent in by the Japanese.

All day long the party sat around waiting, keeping out of sight of the many fishing boats which now dotted the sea off the beach, and feeling the hours drag by interminably. About midday they had another moment of fear when a Japanese cruiser came in sight, steaming slowly north and close inshore. Again they wondered if the operation had become known to the Japanese and whether the warship was linked with the Malays who had landed. At last it moved slowly out of sight and the tension relaxed a little.

John Cross was carrying Major Hart's report and some films in a waterproof bag and the latter now briefed him on additional detailed information which he had not included in the written report and which he wanted Cross to transmit verbally to Allied HQ in Ceylon. The two men got on well and Cross wished, not for the first time, that Hart was coming out with them in the submarine. He could not know, when they said goodbye, that he would never see him again.*

During the afternoon Cross noticed that the sea in front of them was swarming with junks and fishing boats. He asked Hart how the submarine was going to get through them without being detected. However, Hart had taken part in beach reconnaissance from naval vessels on previous occasions and was not unduly worried. He was confident that the submarine was lying submerged well offshore and was watching the beach and the fishing craft through the periscope. He thought that the small boats might even be helpful in showing the way through any minefields.

Unknown to the watchers on the beach, but exactly as Hart surmised, the submarine that had come to pick them up was even then lying, submerged and motionless, a few miles offshore. Her captain, Lieutenant-Commander Alastair Mars DSO, DSC, RN†, had carried out a similar operation at this very spot five months before; but that did not make the waiting any less tense. Through the periscope he could see the yellow flag flying in the 'All clear' position: he also saw the flotilla of fishing boats bobbing about between himself and the beach. And he watched the Japanese cruiser steam slowly past. He was not unduly perturbed: these jobs rarely went without a hitch. Last time they had been approached by a patrol-boat, and in trying to escape her attentions, had run into a minefield and got

* When Cross reached India he learned that Hart was very ill with fever. However, he recovered, and was awarded the DSO for his Intelligence work. Later he achieved his ambition to go back to his beloved Java. But the Javanese refused to accept Dutch rule again after the war and Hart was killed by the very people to whom he had devoted his life.
† Mars describes the operation in his book *HMS Thule Intercepts*, Pan Books, 1958.

a mooring wire round one of the propellers. Never a dull moment, in fact. This time they would be constrained by moonrise, soon after 11 pm. He wanted to be clear before that; it would be fairly tight.

He gave his orders to Captain Onslow, Royal Marine Commandos, who was in charge of the landing flotilla of rubber boats. They were to leave the submarine at 8 pm and return, having completed their mission, by 10 pm, leaving an hour in hand for getting clear. Onslow was worried about the number of fishing boats, but Mars thought most of them would probably have gone away by dusk, and that the submarine's conning tower would simply be mistaken for one of them. There was nothing left to do now but watch and wait.

As evening drew on, the beach became a scene of reunions. Throughout the day the guerrillas had patrolled to north and south of it, guarding against any surprise attacks. Now they knew they were safe, as the Japanese could not possibly get there across country in the dark, so they all converged on the beach. Many familiar faces were present; Lee Boon had left his Sakai pupils at Tengkil and had been appointed interpreter to a British officer of Force 136, who now accompanied him. Lee Boon said that when Cross's party had left the Sakai camp those who remained had felt very sad, and old Liu Chin Hung had broken down and wept openly. 'Charlie' was also present, and he told Cross about the heroic death of Ah Kow, a guerrilla friend, who had recently been cornered in a hut by a Japanese patrol. He had fired off all his ammunition and thrown his last grenade before they were able to rush in and kill him.

Jim was busy saying goodbye to all his Chinese friends, including his long-time companion 'Janker Wallah' who had been with him since 1943. As they shook hands he said, 'Selamat jalan' (Go in safety). Then, glancing nervously over his shoulder at the Communist guerrillas, he added, 'Saya banyak takut dia' (I fear them very much). He said that, as soon as the war ended, he would leave the jungle and return to Singapore.

It was a wrench to part from this man of another race whom he had come to know so well, and Jim wondered what the future held for these non-Communist Chinese who had thrown in their lot with the guerrillas. Would they really be allowed to go back to their former lives, when the Communists were already planning to resist the returning British? In spite of all that he had suffered in the jungle, and his desperate longing to go home, Jim felt deep emotional ties with the country and with its people.

Cross felt the same, and he was making arrangements to keep in touch with 'Charlie' by an exchange of addresses when suddenly a signal rocket shot up from one of the fishing boats and illuminated the scene. All the tensions of the morning immediately returned. What could it mean? As the various possibilities flashed through their minds they feared, above all, that the submarine might have seen it too and have decided not to come in that night.

An anxious hour of darkness dragged slowly by. Then Hart told Cross to light the rubber flares which had been set out on the beach on sticks. As the first flares flickered and died, Cross lit two more; but still nothing happened. By now the sky was beginning to lighten, heralding the moonrise. Hart said quietly, 'I think you've had it. They won't come in now.'

The disappointment was hard to take. Hart said they should keep the rendezvous for two more nights and then assume that the submarine had been lost and go back to camp. As she would be keeping wireless silence it might be some time before he learned what had gone wrong. Meanwhile Cross could light one final set of flares before they left the beach.

Out in the darkness of the bay, Mars saw the flares burn up, flicker for a time, and die. The fishing boats had thinned out; there were no patrol boats to be seen. He gave the order to surface and HMS *Thule* began to move quietly in towards the beach. Then suddenly they found themselves once again surrounded by fishing boats. Mars ordered both engines to be stopped and for a while they lay silent, watching and listening.

But the timing of the operation was critical and as soon as they had begun to move forward again Mars ordered the dinghies to be brought up, inflated and launched alongside. He told Onslow that all the boats would have to go in together, instead of in flights as planned, to ensure that they got to the beach before the moon was up.

To the party ashore the bay seemed dark and apparently deserted. If the submarine had ever made it this far, something must have gone wrong. They resigned themselves to a second night of waiting, and a third, followed by a return to camp and probably weeks or months before the operation could be laid on again.

About 9 pm, Hart said, 'We'll give it one final try.' Once more they lit the flares, watched them burn up brightly for a time and gutter out, while they stared and listened. Nothing. Then, hardly daring to believe their ears, they heard the bubbling mutter of outboards – but they were heading in the wrong direction. They listened, appalled and suspicious. The three Malays, the passing cruiser, the unexplained rocket – to men as keyed up as they were, it was blindingly obvious.

'Japs!' someone whispered hoarsely, and they dashed into the cover of the jungle, weapons cocked, waiting. The boats had altered course. Now they could make them out, several lashed together, heading straight for them. The sound of the engines stopped abruptly; then the Marines, led by Captain Onslow, jumped ashore and hauled the dinghies up.

By then Hart and the rest had come stumbling out from behind the trees, to help Onslow and his marines who were hard at work unloading the six tons of weapons and stores. Confusion and babel ensued as the excited guerrillas grabbed all they could and made off into the jungle.

The escapees quickly said goodbye and handed over their weapons to those remaining behind. Jim parted reluctantly with his newly-acquired Sten gun and also with the red blanket which had been such a boon to him over the past two years. He slipped off his jungle boots and gave them away too; after years of going barefoot or in rubber sandals he was really happier without them.

As soon as the beach was clear of stores Onslow gave the order to embark. The American pilot, John Cross, Jim and Brian got into one dinghy and were soon speeding across the water, guided by the Commandos who were using special glasses to home in on an infra-red beacon mounted on the bridge of the submarine.

Cross looked back at the receding coast, the dark line of the jungle contrasting with the silvery sea. This view, he thought, might appear enticing and romantic to a tourist on a cruise liner, but he had no such illusions nor any regrets at leaving it.

Jim also surveyed the disappearing jungle, his home for three and a quarter long years. Now that his escape had become a reality instead of a dream, he was trembling all over and his heart was beating fast.

As they drew near to *Thule* they saw that she was lying stern-on to the shore and they could hear her engines throbbing, charging the batteries before diving. In another minute they were alongside and being hauled aboard by strong hands and hustled below. The rubber boats were slashed and sunk with lumps of pig-iron. Then Mars nosed the submarine cautiously out of the bay. They were on their way.

At that moment an enemy patrol-boat appeared, clearly visible in the moonlight, between them and deep water. The gunners tensed; they could sink her if they had to, but that might jeopardize the party ashore. The patrol-boat came ahead, idling along with intolerable slowness as *Thule* edged her way out of the bay. Everyone breathed again.

Then somebody glanced astern; one of the dinghies had failed to sink and sat there, bobbing gently on the calm surface of the bay, an all too vivid sign of their visit. Cursing, Mars went astern, and, as it came alongside, the First Lieutenant, held by his heels, leant over the casing and at last succeeded in despatching it to the bottom. The patrol-boat had now crossed ahead.

Once again Mars rang for 'Slow ahead' and HM Submarine *Thule* started to gather way, to thread through the minefields and set course for Fremantle. For Jim, the long struggle for survival was really over at last.

Epilogue

The old familiar Norfolk countryside seemed unchanged to Jim, as the train from Liverpool Street trundled towards Norwich, and this added to the turmoil of his emotions. These pictures – stubblefield and woodland, still water and wide skies – had continued to shine, fragmentary and vivid, at the back of his mind throughout the years he had been away, a source of strength and resolution, yet utterly remote and unattainable. Now, here he was, travelling through them. The scene was as he remembered it, but he saw it now through a confusing screen of experience and he felt bewildered and a little afraid.

In the two months since he and Cross and the others had scrambled aboard *Thule* in that silvered and sinister bay, they had found the process of adapting to civilization more of a strain than they were prepared for. The voyage in the submarine, relatively uneventful except for an encounter with another, which turned out to be British, had been a novel enough way to pass back through the looking-glass and into a dazzling world of lights, hot baths, comfortable beds, abundant food and drink, and their own gaunt reflections in the mirror.

From Australia they had finally trailed home by way of Ceylon and India, Jim to be interrogated by a rather bored Captain in the War Office, at last to be deposited at Liverpool Street station by two MPs. He had been parted from all his companions, the last props of his bizarre jungle life knocked away and, as yet, nothing but this view from the carriage window to replace them.

No one had thought to tell his parents when he would be

arriving, and he had had no opportunity to do so himself; so he searched in vain for a familiar face at Norwich Thorpe station. There was none. Nor was there a train that night on to Cawston. Philosophically Jim curled up in a corner of the empty carriage and cat-napped. At dawn he caught the newspaper train home.

It was too early for taxis and too far to walk, but by chance he saw on the platform an old pal of his, John Knights, who was on leave from the R.A.F. and he gave Jim a lift. The car had barely stopped before his mother, who had been on watch ever since receiving Jim's telegram on his arrival in England, rushed out and threw her arms round him with a stifled sob of joy. His father simply stared at him, then, overcome with emotion, turned and went into the house. So, unheralded and by a chance lift from a friend, Jim Wright came home at last.

A few months after Jim's return the survivors of the 6th Norfolks also came home, many of them in very poor shape although their sufferings while prisoners of the Japanese had bound them together in a strong comradeship. But Jim felt a stranger to them and avoided their company, concerned only to forget his knife-edge life in Malaya and the deaths of his friends.

This was easier when the nightmares which disfigured his sleep became less frequent; easier still when, during a spell in hospital, he met, and later married, a childhood friend, Kathie Payne. With patience and understanding she helped to submerge that haunting past with a tranquil present.

In 1948 Malaya caught his interest again when the Chinese communists launched their campaign of terrorism to drive out the British and gain control of the country. Jim was not surprised; he remembered how keen the communists had been to lay their hands on weapons although they had used them little against the Japanese. Nevertheless, it grieved him deeply; many of them had been his close friends. He did not condone their acts of terrorism but he knew that, if he had been required to do so, he could not willingly have fought against these men whose salt he had eaten and to whom his life was forfeit.

Gradually his bouts of malaria grew fewer; and then he went back to hospital, this time for a year, during which he nearly died. After his recovery he became once more simply a part of Cawston life, albeit a little solitary and withdrawn. But he was not fit enough to go back to his job on the Heydon estate;

instead he worked a Council small-holding and later became caretaker at the local school. He was, he felt, as happy as he was likely or had any right to be. But, however far the past receded, the memory of all those who had not had his luck lay across his spirit like the shadow of a thundercloud across the Heydon stubbles. Nevertheless he was content enough.

Then, in 1970, out of the blue, came an opportunity to fly out to Singapore to stay with Kathie's niece and her RAF husband. To go or not to go, that was the question. Kathie was against it, remembering the nightmares; but Jim realized that, deep down where memories too sharply engraved to be erased still stirred, he desperately wanted to return. The need lay beyond rational thought or explanation: it was more like an act of faith.

So they went. And, as it turned out, that journey made it possible later on for Jim to call up in minute detail the experiences recorded in this book. Their aircraft arrived over Johore late in the afternoon, and Jim looked down in wonderment at the almost unbroken carpet of green. This, he thought, was what those Japanese pilots had seen as they flew over the jungle on reconnaissance: little wonder that they had so rarely seen anything. He and his companions had been as invisible as ants in long grass to a gardener. Did the ants know they could not be seen, though?

After a day or two in Singapore Jim hired a car and, with Kathie's niece and her husband, drove over that fateful causeway across the Straits, into Johore and a past of almost thirty years ago. As they drove north, the names came back vividly to Jim, but the vividness was of memory: their force, in this restored and peaceful country, was spent. Man, ever renewing his ravaged heritage, man and the jungle had seen to that. Yet, changed as it all was, Jim felt that, somehow, by his return he was keeping faith with all those comrades whose graves the jungle had utterly obliterated and whose only memorial was a name on an official casualty list – and his own remembrance of them. He could think of them – Douglas and Fred, Tom and Hector and the rest – with sadness still, but without the bitter grief of former times.

His final journey into Johore took him to Rengit. Amazingly, the water-tower where it had all begun, was still standing and he stopped the car and wandered over to it. Few people now, he thought, would realize what those chips and patches meant.

He strolled on down a wide track which led eventually to the jungle. A fallen tree lay beside it and he sat down on this and lit a cigarette. Here nothing had changed; the sounds and smells of the jungle were as he had known them and, as he sat listening, he gradually felt a return of that prickling of awareness and fear.

Suddenly a lorryload of young workmen in white singlets came grinding along the track and, in that instant, while his thoughts were enmeshed in the past, he felt a strong urge to dive for cover. 'Idiot!' he murmured to himself as he watched it pass. There were no *Japun* now.

A party of villagers led by an elderly Chinese came down the track from the water-tower. They stopped, looking curiously at him, and Jim suddenly found himself remembering odd phrases of the Malay which he had not thought of or needed for twenty-five years.

'I was here in the war,' he managed to say. 'I was wounded,' he pointed to his foot, 'and spent many days wandering alone.'

'You were lucky not to die,' said the old Chinese. 'Many soldiers died, or were killed by the *Japun*.'

One of the men started talking excitedly to the old man. 'He says that, when he was a child, he was in a *kampong* near here, and he remembers a soldier with a wounded foot coming there. Perhaps it was you.'

'It could have been,' Jim said; and it was as if past and present had come together to make of experience a perfect circle.

'You were lucky not to die,' said the old man again. 'Many, many, women and children too, were killed. Those were bad times. But all that is past now. Now the country is peaceful and prosperous. You fought for the good which we enjoy.'

Jim sat for a moment in silence, thinking of the many Chinese who had helped him in his fight for survival and a wonderful feeling of peace suddenly flowed into his mind.

It was time to go; rising to his feet he said goodbye to the old man and walked back towards the road. After a minute he turned round to have a last look at the jungle. The Chinese were still standing in a group, motionless, watching him go. He raised a hand to them and they waved back crying, '*Selamat jalan*'.

'Selamat tinggal. Terima kaseh' (Goodbye and thank you) Jim
shouted back and turning, went slowly up the track to the car.

For that encounter alone, this journey into the past had been
worth making.

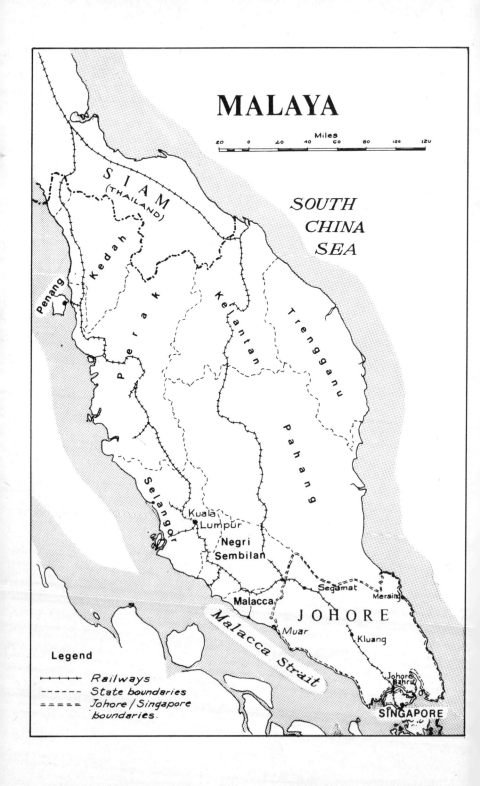

MALAYA

Miles

20   0   20   40   60   80   100   120

SOUTH
CHINA
SEA

S I A M
(THAILAND)

Kedah

Penang

Perak

Kelantan

Trengganu

Pahang

Selangor

Kuala
Lumpur

Negri
Sembilan

Segamat

Mersing

Malacca

JOHORE

Muar

Kluang

Malacca Strait

Johore
Bahru

SINGAPORE

Legend

Railways

State boundaries

Johore / Singapore
boundaries.

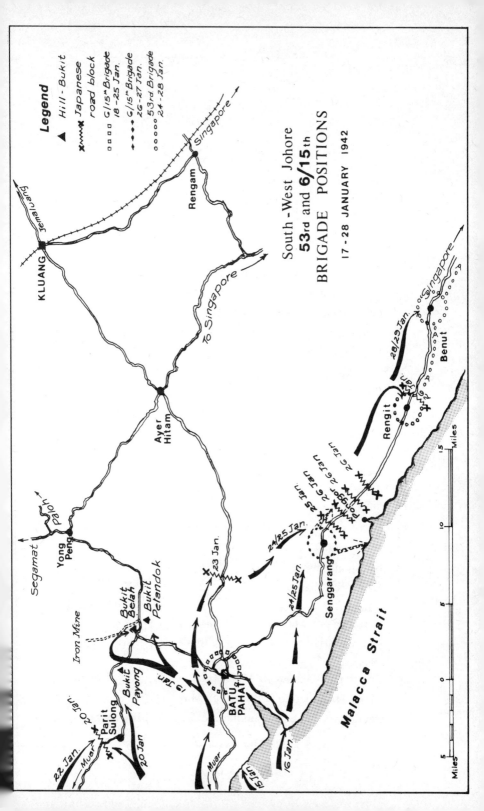

South-West Johore 53rd and 6/15th BRIGADE POSITIONS

17 - 28 JANUARY 1942

Legend

▲ Hill - Bukit
✕✕✕✕ Japanese road block
□ □ □ □ 6/15ᵗʰ Brigade 18-25 Jan.
• • • • 6/15ᵗʰ Brigade 26-27 Jan.
○ ○ ○ ○ 53rd Brigade 24-28 Jan.

KEY TO MAP

1 Rengit water tower.
2 Japanese ambushes (29 & 31 January 1942).
3 40th milestone.
4 Guerrilla camp (3–25 March 1942).
5 Soldiers' camp (25 March–mid-April 1942).
6 Layang Layang.
7 Tak Wah Heng.
8 Poh Lee Sen.
9 'Death Shack' camp (early December 1942–April 1943).
10 Kampong Rantau Panjang (April–May 1943).
11 Kuala Sisek.
12 Kampong Tengkil.
13 Area of Barry & Cross's camps, Tengkil (31 May 1943–17 April 1944 and mid-August 1944–March 1945).
14 Barry's ill-fated expedition (18 April 1944).
15 Kampong Danau.
16 Kampong Lubok Pusing.
17 Kuala Kambau.
18 Camp. Barry's suicide (3 July 1944). Guest's death (13 July 1944). Gooch's death (19 July 1944).
19 Jim and Brian Smith return to Cross's camp (early August 1944).
20 British party set out for Major Hart's camp (1 April 1945).
21 Major Hart's camp (17 April–27 May 1945).
22 Rendezvous with HM Submarine *Thule* (31 May 1945).

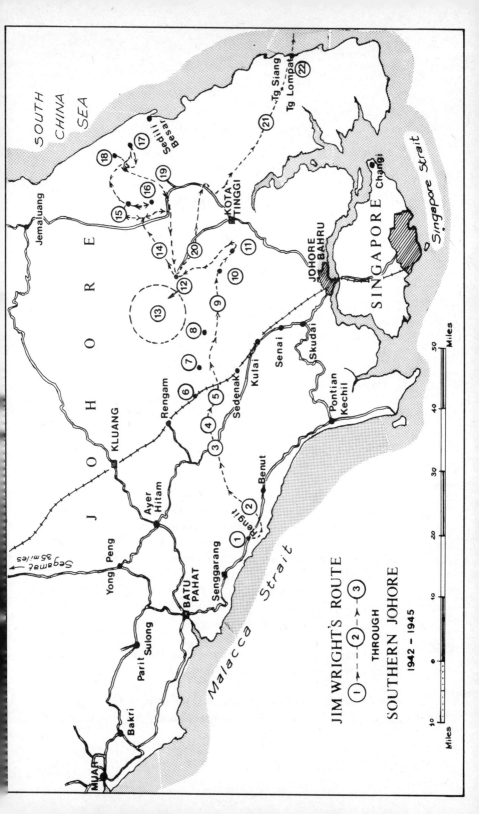

JIM WRIGHT'S ROUTE

① --- ② →→→ ③

THROUGH

SOUTHERN JOHORE

1942 – 1945

APPENDIX

List of Identified Soldiers in Jim Wright's Camps, 1942–1945

Sources

a. AIF Battalion Associations – 2/19th and 2/29th.
b. British Battalion Associations – 6. R. Norfolk and 2 Loyals.
c. Commonwealth War Graves Commission – England and Australia.
d. Department of Veterans' Affairs – Australia.
e. Imperial War Museum – papers of the late CQMS John Cross DCM.
f. Evidence of three living survivors – E. J. Wright, H. J. Crowe and D. H. Robertson AIF.

Numbers of men.

There is, inevitably, after a passage of forty years, some disagreement among survivors regarding both the number of men in the camps and the dates of some events. No survivor has been able to remember, or perhaps ever knew, more than a few names, and these were often Christian or nicknames only.

Wright says there were 21 men when he arrived in March, 1942, and that five more joined later (total 26).

Crowe gives the number as 'about 20' plus another 5 later (total 25).

Robertson says that when his party of 5 joined early in June, 1942, the total was 18, but he was not aware that 5 had previously left the camp (total 23).

Papers of the late John Cross name only 21 men. Cross was not in the camps and his only information came from Brian Smith, and then not until 1944. Cross also gave Army numbers and initials against the names. Such details were certainly not kept in the camps by Brian Smith or by anyone else and I can only assume that Cross obtained these details from the Australian authorities when he was debriefed on his way home, and entered them in his records against the names Smith had given to him. Both Cross and Smith are now dead.

After careful study of the evidence of the three living survivors I am of the opinion that there were between 23 and 26 men in the camps at one time or another. In spite of exhaustive research I have not been able to name any more than 21. Crowe and Wright have been shown lists of all AIF who have no known grave and who were killed or missing during the second half of January, 1942, but neither were able to add to the 21 names.

I have therefore taken Wright's 26 as being the maximum. He was in the camps until all AIF had died whereas Crowe was there only from March 1942, and Robertson from June 1942, until they left together at the end of November 1942.

Dates of Death (see list overleaf).
Against the names of identified men I have shown the official dates of death (which were taken from John Cross's reports after the war). Wright does not agree with several of these and both he and Crowe disagree with the sequence of events as contained in the Cross papers. In the text of the story I have, therefore, kept to Wright's memory of events and dates, amended, where he has agreed, by the evidence of Crowe and Robertson.

Robert Hamond.

Number	Names	Rank	Unit
1. vx42142	DAY, Frederick Allan	Pte	2/29th BN AIF ⎫
2. vx56460	OPIE, William Charles	Pte	2/29th Bn AIF ⎬
3. vx55873	DEAN, Frederick Victor	Pte	2/29th Bn AIF. ⎭
4. vx39208	CROFT, Ronald Frederick	Sgt	2/29th Bn. AIF. ⎫
5. vx60111	FLOWER, Raymond Harold George	Pte	2/29th Bn AIF. ⎬
6. vx34966	NIPPARD, Francis Patrick Daniel	Pte	2/29th Bn. AIF. ⎫
7. vx34978	NIPPARD, Edward Peter	Pte	2/29th Bn AIF. ⎭
8. vx55565	RAE, Stanley Maxwell	Pte	2/29th Bn. AIF.
9. ?	?	?	? ? AIF.
10. ?	?	?	? ? AIF.
11. 5773431	CROWE, Henry Joseph	Pte	6 R. Norfolk.
12. NX42702	ROBERTSON, Donald Henry	Pte	2/19th Bn AIF.
13. ?	?	?	? ? AIF.
14. ?	?	?	? ? AIF.
15. vx36094	ANDERSON, Sydney Robert Thomas	Pte	2/29th Bn. AIF.
16. vx27314	CONOLE, Mac (or Max)	Pte	2/29th Bn AIF.
17. vx35703	BROOKER, Aubrey Cecil	Pte	2/29th Bn AIF.
18. 3855834	SHOWELL, Thomas	L/Sgt	2 Loyals
19. vx45880	PICKERING, Arnold Thomas Henry	Pte	2/29th Bn AIF.
20. ?	?	?	? ? AIF.
21. vx44228	ALDERSEA, Jack	Pte	2/29th Bn AIF.
22. vx55057	STEPHENS, Hector Charles	Pte	2/29th Bn AIF.
23. 5771548	GUEST, Douglas George	Pte	6 R. Norfolk
24. 5781804	GOOCH, Frederick Robert	Pte	6 R. Norfolk
25. 3866136	SMITH, Brian Osborne	Pte	2 Loyals
26. 5776863	WRIGHT, Ernest James	Pte	6 R. Norfolk

Died	Remarks
26. 5.42.	Left camp 14.4.42. Killed by a Jap patrol or captured and executed after interrogation. OPIE served under the name of W. C. Erwin.
15. 4.42.	Date of death is wrong. Left camp 26.4.42. Probably captured and shot at Johore Bahru between 26.4 and 24.11.
31.10.42.	Brothers – Frank and George.
4.11.42	Brothers – Frank and George.
18.11.42.	Called Max.
?	
?	
Survived.	Captured December 42. Sent to Changi. Alive 1983.
Survived.	'Curly'. Escaped from Changi March 42. Joined camp early June 42. Left with Crowe. Sent to Japan 1944. Alive 1983.
?	
?	
3. 1.43.	
3. 1.43.	
11. 1.43.	
14. 2.43.	
24. 2.43.	Called Bill.
?	Called Allan or Alan.
17. 3.43.	Jim says the only Jack he knew died in December 1942.
31. 5.43.	Died on stretcher en route to guerrilla camp at Tengkil.
3. 7.44.	Date should be 13.7.44. At Kambau, East Johore.
19. 7.44.	At Kambau.
Survived.	Died 15.11.52. Reason not known.
Survived.	Alive 1983.

Other Camps

Known to John Cross but not to Jim Wright and his comrades, there was another group of officers and men spread over various camps in northern Johore. A survivor, ex-Sergeant Arthur Shephard, 2/29th Battalion AIF, has given me the details below.

vx39035	Lieut	R. M. McLURE, 2/4 Anti Tank Regt RAA	Survived
vx38587	Gnr	C. V. BROWN, 2/4 Anti Tank Regt RAA	Died of wounds 4.2.42.
vx39088*	Sgt	A. F. SHEPHARD, 2/29th Bn AIF	Survived
vx48213	Cpl	H. R. RYAN, 2/29th Bn AIF	Survived
vx35020	Sigmn	G. WAINWRIGHT, 2/29th Bn AIF	Died 29.4.43.
vx34900	Pte	T. J. H. PERCIVAL, 2/29th Bn AIF	Died 28.7.43.
vx47219	Pte	R. J. ROACH, 2/29th Bn AIF	Died 6.4.45.
2979955*	Pte	D. STEWART, 2 Argylls	Survived
2979828*†	Pte	J. BENNETT, 2 Argylls	Survived
10394	Rfmn	GAJE SING SANKRYAL, Garhwal Rifles	Survived
	Pte	SMIT TONSEA MATOENGKAS, Marechaussees	Died
225852	Lieut	T. M. SMYLLIE, Chief of Police, Kedah	Died 21.3.43
225885	2/Lieut	M. P. BARLOW, Planter, Malacca	Died 28.4.43.
225851	2/Lieut	A. E. SCOTT-SKOVSO, 1st Feltartilleriregiment Denmark (SIS Agent?)	Died 8.7.43.
225847	2/Lieut	L. H. W. TAYLOR, Planter, Ipoh	Died 17.7.45.
*	?	J. M. COTTERILL, Planter, Sungei Lembing, Kuantan	Survived

* Alive in 1980
*† Bennett was with this party for only part of his time in the jungle.

One Gurkha officer and three riflemen of 2/1st Gurkha Rifles also joined Chinese guerrillas (area unspecified) and fought with them against the Japanese until rescued by Force 136 in July 1945. (*Eastern Epic, Vol I*, Compton Mackenzie, Chatto and Windus, 1951).

Bibliography

Louis Allen, *Singapore 1941–42* Davis-Poynter, London
Noel Barber, *Sinister Twilight* Collins, London
Noel Barber, *The War of the Running Dogs* Collins, London
Lt-Gen H. Gordon Bennett (late GOC AIF Malaya) *Why Singapore Fell* Angus & Robertson, Sydney & London
Russell Braddon *The Naked Island* Great Pan Illustrated
Kate Caffery *Out in the Midday Sun* Andre Deutsch, London
F. Spencer Chapman *The Jungle is Neutral* Chatto & Windus, London
John Cross, DCM *Red Jungle* Robert Hale & Co, London
Capt. C. G. T. Dean, MBE *The Loyal Regiment 1919–1953* Wm Brendon & Son Ltd, Mayflower Press, Watford
Stanley Falk *Seventy Days to Singapore* Robert Hale, London 1975
P. K. Kemp *The Royal Norfolk Regiment 1919–1951 Vol. III* Soman Wherry Press, Norwich
James Leasor *Singapore, the Battle that Changed the World* Hodder & Stoughton 1968
Compton Mackenzie *Eastern Epic Vol. 1* Chatto & Windus, 1951
Alastair Mars, DSO, DSC & Bar *HMS Thule Intercepts* Pan Books 1958
Frank Owen *The Fall of Singapore* Pan Illustrated
Lt Gen A. E. Percival, CB, DSO, OBE, MC *The War in Malaya* Eyre & Spottiswood, London
Lord Russell of Liverpool *The Knights of Bushido* Corgi
Brigadier Ivan Simson (formerly Chief Engineer, Malaya Command) *Singapore: To Little, Too Late* Leo Cooper, London
Brigadier The Rt Hon Sir John Smyth Bt, VC, MC *Leadership in War, 1939–45* David & Charles
Arthur Swinson *Four Samurai* Hutchinson, London

Ian Trenowden *Operations Most Secret SOE: The Malayan Theatre* William Kimber London 1978

Masanobu Tsuji *Singapore* Constable, London

Major-Gen S. Woodburn-Kirby, CB, CMG, CIE, OBE, MC *Singapore: The Chain of Disaster* Cassell, London

The London Gazette 26 February, 1948 HMSO

Unpublished Sources consulted:

6th Battalion, The Royal Norfolk Regiment

   War Diaries, 13 January–17 February 1942

   Report to Army HQ, New Delhi, by Major A. R. Stacy, April 1942

   Nominal Roll, Casualty Lists and War Office Roll of Honour.

Acknowledgements

During the writing of this book many people have given me helpful information. I have been surprised but greatly encouraged by the unstinted help which I have received from many who had no connection with, and perhaps little interest in, the events related in this story. I owe them all my gratitude for their contributions.

I am particularly indebted to the late John Cross DCM, who helped me with my initial research, and to his family who allowed me full access to his war papers which, after his death in 1981, they lodged in the Imperial War Museum.

I also acknowledge to Robert Hale & Company, publishers of John Cross's fascinating book *Red Jungle*, that I have drawn extensively on this book for the periods where John Cross and Jim Wright were together in the jungles of Johore.

In describing the final escape from Malaya by submarine, I am also indebted to Commander Alistair Mars DSO DSC & Bar RN for the details given in his book *HMS Thule Intercepts*, Pan Books, 1958.

For information on military operations I am grateful to the following:

The Royal Norfolk Regiment
Lieutenant Colonels A. B. Cubitt and A. W. J. Turnbull MC (Regimental Secretary), Major A. R. Stacy, CSM M.E. Rudling BEM and ex-private Harry Crowe, a living survivor of the jungle camps in 1942. He has given me valuable supporting evidence of conditions and morale in the camps, until he left in November, 1942, and has identified some of the occupants.

Ex-private Bert Hall, whose chance remark to me five years ago, led me to tell this story.

The Loyal Regiment

The late Colonel P. H. Rogers JP, Major P. A. Mauldon and ex-Sergeant Joe Swarbrick, a personal friend of Tom Showell.

Organisations and Institutions

The following have given me invaluable help in identifying men named in the story, and in tracing the families of those who died in the camps: Headpostmasters of Tredegar, Sutton (Surrey), Swinton, Bletchley, British Telecom Museum, The Passport Office, DHSS Norcross, Editors of Swinton and Pendlebury Journal, Bristol United Press Limited, Sutton and Cheam Advertiser Series, National Federation of Far East Prisoner of War Clubs and Associations, Ray Manning, FEPOWA Norfolk.

The Royal Geographical Society, for help with maps and The Imperial War Museum for releasing information on aircraft and weapons and for making available to me war papers of the late John Cross DCM.

Commonwealth War Graves Commission for help in identifying un-named men.

Australia

Ron Zwar, Department of Veterans' Affairs, Adelaide, and the Office of Australian War Graves, Woden, Colonel J. Hope-Campbell, Charles E. Stuart (State Secretary ex-POW and Relatives Association, Melbourne), Colonel R. W. Newton AM MBE ED (co-Patron 2/19th Battalion Association), R. W. Christie (Hon Sec 2/29th Battalion Association), A. Dandie (Hon. Sec 2/30th Battalion Association) and ex-Sergeant Arthur Shephard, 2/29th Battalion, (a survivor from another jungle camp who sent me a very interesting account of his experiences). Don Robertson ('Curly') whom I traced at the last moment, supplied me with valuable information about his life in the camps.

My knowledge of Malaya is slight and I am grateful to the following for guiding my pen in this respect:

Colonel John Davis CBE DSO (Malayan Police and Force 136), Pauline Godbold (who, as a young girl, Koh Say Nya, lived near Malacca during the Japanese occupation), Captains J. B. Masefield and Forbes Wallace (Malayan Police) and R. C. Barnard (Malayan Forestry Service).

Mrs H. Ireton and Mrs E. Reynolds gave me personal information and photographs of Tom Showell and Fred Gooch. I was unable to trace any living relative of Douglas Guest and Brian Smith's daughter, Mrs M. West, was unwilling to give me any information about her father.

I am deeply grateful to Francis Bennett, Jill Hughes, Leo Cooper and Hugh and Robin Popham for their sound professional advice, critical editing and constant encouragement during the writing of this story. Also to my step-daughter, Tessa Bennett, for suggesting the title.

I would also like to thank Captain R. C. Read CBE FRICS for drawing the maps.

Finally, I am greatly indebted to Kathie Wright who, despite her earlier misgivings, encouraged and helped Jim to write his story in a correct sequence of events, and to my wife who has given me much encouragement and has patiently endured the research and writing of this book over the past five years.

Robert Hamond